T0156948

INFORMATION AGE TALES

INFORMATION
AGE
TALES

BRAD BRADFORD

From Adam's Apple to the Apple II and Beyond

Foreword and Epilogue by eBook Inventor Michael S. Hart

iUniverse, Inc.
Bloomington

Information Age Tales
From Adam's Apple to the Apple II and Beyond

iUniverse books may be ordered through booksellers or by contacting:

iUniverse
1663 Liberty Drive
Bloomington, IN 47403
www.iuniverse.com
1-800-Authors (1-800-288-4677)

ISBN: 978-1-4620-3047-7 (sc)
ISBN: 978-1-4620-3182-5 (hc)
ISBN: 978-1-4620-3048-4 (e)

Library of Congress Control Number: 2011910889

Printed in the United States of America

iUniverse rev. date: 08/19/2011

Dedication

to

CAROL

For becoming my smart, beautiful bride in 1949
and then giving fully of herself to me and our wonderful
family incomparable love, care, feeding, fun, and friendship.
Also for her perceptive editing of my copy over many
decades, especially during the writing of this book.

Epigraph

*Neither to persuade nor indoctrinate but rather
to foster curiosity about past Information Technology.*

*Paraphrased from Henry Hobhouse's
introduction to* Seeds of Change.

Table of Contents

Foreword

by Michael S. Hart, founder of Project Gutenberg and inventor of eBooks

What millions call "the greatest story ever told" opens in John 1 with the simple phrase: "In the beginning was the word—"

This book also begins with that wondrous first Information Technology and then moves on to tales about the wonders of the written word—great stories, many of them likely new to most readers. In them, you'll find all the backgrounds, foregrounds, premises, conclusions, and surprises that make up the best and most valuable books.

At eighty-nine, Brad Bradford brings a long lifetime of experience in newspapers during the hot-metal-type era and in the initial transition to digital phototypesetting.

At sixty-four, I bring another full lifetime lived both at that exact moment where my experiences could straddle working in print shops and in the current digital eBook era..

My degree in human-computer interfaces in 1973 led to my appointment as adjunct professor at Benedictine University, where I built the world's first electronic library in 1988.

You could walk into that library, and the first thing you'd see was the computer asking if there were any books you wanted. You selected books from our early selections and then inserted a floppy disc. Then you were prompted to close the drive door, and you got your books. No waiting.

No overdue fines. Never any lost books. You could search books using the SEARCH function on your own computer, import quotations into paper e-mails, etc., and copy the book.

Reading forward or backward

Before we go any further, a very personal suggestion:

My own way of reading this book, including the Foreword and Epilogue, would be to read it backward, to jump to the start of the Epilogue.

This is because my own perspective on the history of the written word is tied so powerfully to the history of eBooks—the most recent method of publishing words—and I would work back from there, because I like to start with a foundation I understand and know from my own personal experience.

In addition, I find that reading books backward, even difficult college textbooks, organizes material in a way which most college students find foreign, but one to which I owe a great deal. I doubt I would have done nearly as well if I had read those books in the normal manner. I wouldn't have remembered the beginning by the time I had gotten to the end.

This book is important enough that I want you to remember one end and remember it well by the time you get to the other end.

My own personal perspective ranges from the Gutenberg Press to eBooks. It nicely complements Mr. Bradford's perspective that gives weight—well-deserved weight—to portions of history he has pulled out from shadows of the past.

Mr. Bradford starts with the oldest possible perspective of the word and proceeds through the ages up to his own unique experiences with Gutenberg typography and Mergenthaler's wondrous Linotype machine, which allowed for the unprecedented expansion of publishing in the twentieth century before he led his paper's switch to digital phototype.

My own personal experience picks up shortly before his left off, working in a university print shop that made textbooks with offset machines and a new variety of mimeograph that duplicated the original to make the master copy.

From "publication" to "public-ation."

Each of our perspectives tells the stories of how publication changed to a more public-ation, as the public shared more and more of that which an elite class had only previously been privy to.

Before the Gutenberg Press, literacy rates were only one percent at most, and reading materials were available only to a privileged few. Today, the common person can buy a desktop-terabyte drive for fifty dollars and a pocket-terabyte drive for a hundred dollars—drives that can hold a million book titles in plain text or 2.5 million in compressed text.

Such modern information technologies offer you a chance to learn how your world has been changed more than you might have ever guessed. They offer access to an entertaining and informative series of examples of how the word and particularly the printed word have been used. They can let you move from the peoples of ancient eras, such as the Sumerians, Egyptians, Greeks, and Romans, on to those of the French, Germans, English, and eventually worldwide public-ations.

The doorway is right in front of you. All you have to do is open it.

Knowledge is power.
—Francis Bacon

Expanding the sharing of knowledge upset the
balance of power and spawned revolutionary
changes in civilization after civilization.
—brad bradford

Preface

Way back in the fifteenth century a man named Johann Gutenberg invented the "printing press." More than 400 years passed before Ottmar Mergenthaler found a way in the late 1880s to mechanize that historic invention.

Then, less than a century later – in the 1980s – digital printing displaced Mergenthaler's wondrous Linotypes..

Today, you belong to a tiny minority if you recognized the name Mergenthaler, and an even smaller minority if you are aware of his Linotype's historic importance.

This book germinated from seeds planted in the 1930s when a junior high print shop class introduced me to Gutenberg's invention. There, the "pick and click" of the type in the stick immediately captivated me.

During the heyday of Linotypes—from the late 1940s into the late 1980s—I worked at city editor and managing editor jobs which often sent me into composing rooms filled with those towering, typesetting machines' clickety-clacks and the acrid odors from their melting pots of metal.

As the current Information Technology revolution got underway, those experiences set me looking into the hidden history of information technologies that preceded the present Age of Cyberspace.

My most surprising discovery was that the wedding of *information* and *technology* took place when our Homo sapiens ancestors first made their appearance on this planet.

Somehow, that couple kept its marriage secret while cohabitating and upsetting power balances on this planet for thousands of years. In fact, the term "information technology" remained unused until almost the end of the twentieth century.

Published in 1984, my *Webster's Ninth New Collegiate Dictionary* still treated them as singles, defining *information* on page 620 and *technology* on page 1,211.

(On page 621, it lists *information science* immediately before *information theory*. There's no definition of *information technology* between them.)

In its 2011 online dictionary, however, *Merriam-Webster* defines INFORMATION TECHNOLOGY as "the technology involving the development, maintenance, and use of computer systems, software, and networks for the processing and distribution of data."

According to *M-W*, the first known coupling of those two words was in 1978, the same year I bought the Apple II desktop computer that introduced me to modern Information Technology.

Aware that owners of Apple II desktop computers might have learned something about digital word processing, the bosses at the *Kalamazoo Gazette* sat this then city editor in front of a keyboard linked digitally to a cathode ray tube (CRT), a monitor similar to ones found in early TV sets.

I could write and edit copy on this setup. One key click punched holes in paper tapes that—when run through apparatus in the back shop—set type twice as fast on a Linotype as a printer could keyboard it.

Writing a book to sound a Paul Revere-type alarm warning that digital InfoTech would change the world suddenly seemed like a good idea. The revolution's rapid pace, howerer, soon made the public fully aware of its impact. Besides, limited technical background ruled out my trying to write such a book.

So in spare time during my remaining working years at the *Gazette* and in retirement, curiosity prompted notes randomly taken and linked to history trails recalled from high school and college studies.

Especially rewarding were sweeping histories, such as *The Rise of the West: A History of the Human Community* by William H. McNeill, Daniel

L. Boorstin's *The Discoverers: A History of Man's Search to Know His World and Himself,* and Elizabeth L. Einsenstein's specialized epic, *The Printing Press as an Agent of Change: Communications and Cultural Transformations in Early Modern Europe.*

Expanded access to wasted intellect
Feeding my curiosity with random research convinced me of the following:

- Earlier InfoTech revolutionaries opened knowledge access to larger and larger segments of the population that put to use previously wasted intellect.
- In each case, they expanded sharing the power of knowing. [1]
- The InfoTech trail began with the first Homo sapiens, then moved on to evolutions and revolutions that upset the power balance in one civilization after another.
- Pioneer leaders of today's ongoing information technology revolution marched in firm footprints implanted by earlier InfoTech revolutionaries.

More than a million words piled up in my Macintosh hard drives before the process of condensing them into this book began about five yeas ago.

The book's purpose remains as stated in its epigraph is as follows:

*Neither to persuade nor indoctrinate—rather
to foster curiosity about past InfoTech.*

Nothing would make the result more rewarding than for a scholar (or scholars) to take freely from this book whatever might be useful and write a more complete, traditional history.

---

1   1a: the power of knowing as distinguished from the power to feel and to will: the capacity for knowledge—Merriam Webster

Intriguing discoveries along the InfoTech trail

Trekking the InfoTech trail in chapters ahead will expose you to offbeat tales that include the following:

- "Water monkeys."[2]
- The "goldsmith sire of capitalism."
- Fearsome Mongol warriors playing a positive role in the rise of Western Civilization.
- Interchangeable parts more than four centuries before Eli Whitney won his historic patent to manufacture muskets with them.
- The '49 Gold Rush helping to finance "The Eighth Wonder of the World."
- Mark Twain going bankrupt because he backed a Mergenthaler competitor.

Michael Hart's involvement

In late 2009, an online correspondence began with Michael S. Hart, inventor of the eBook and founder of Project Gutenberg.

Professor Hart agreed to check out a couple of chapter drafts of this book and immediately began suggesting bits of InfoTech history—facts previously unknown to me.

They belonged in the book, but they became so numerous that only a few have been specifically attributed to him.

His discerning input of InfoTech history and skilled copyediting eventually led a request that he write the Foreword and the Epilogue.

2　A high school student—recalling my mention of Aquatic Apes the previous week—wanted to hear more about "those water monkeys."

CHAPTER 1

"I am thoroughly convinced that language evolved out of man's basic need to complain."
—Comedienne Lily Tomlin (1939–)

Did Water Monkeys Swim Before We Spoke?

In the Bible, God's first gift to man isn't a lesson about how to make a fire or fashion a needle, a knife, or a spear. He first blesses him with language. Even before He takes Adam's rib to make Eve, He tells Adam to name every living creature. Adam immediately understands God's words and enunciates his own.

Anthropologists say that our ancestors had been more prey than predator for millions of years before mastering speech and language about fifty thousand years ago. That set Homo sapiens apart from all other species.

Hummingbirds, songbirds, and parrots all produce learned songs. The honeybee finds food, heads back to the hive, then dances on the wall in circles or straight lines to point others to where it's been.

Other birds and beasts make sounds to attract, threaten, or alert each other. Many possess other marvelous skills, such as the ability to navigate across thousands of miles or a sense of smell that penetrates a mile or more.

But only we humans open our mouths and emit intelligible sounds that empower us to share so many types of knowledge.

When we speak, we can:

- Describe past events
- Forecast events
- Recall places and actions far removed
- Abstract, generalize, and synthesize.

Fully articulated speech let our ancestors share the knowledge that helped them control fire and master the tools that enabled our species dominate this planet.

Harmonizing seamless sound waves

Speaking is a very complex process:

- We contract muscles to squeeze the rib cage and push air out from our lungs through the windpipe (trachea).
- Then the air enters the tube-like voice box (larynx) that lies well below the back of the tongue.
- There, the air flows up between the vocal cords to produce a buzzing sound that becomes the voice.
- A resonator in the throat (pharynx) shapes one's voice pattern.
- Finally, tongue and lips form speech in the mouth's oral cavity.

Lungs, voice box, throat, tongue, and lips must all work in the closest harmony to send seamless sound waves in rapid-fire coordination. We can do that about ten times faster than any sounds-within-sounds that chimpanzees make.

The wondrous nature of listening

It's not just the act of speaking that's wondrous.

As we listen, we easily hallucinate word boundaries.

No spaces—such as we use in writing—separate spoken words. Yet beginning as babes, we assimilate the knowledge to make sense of speech.

(Schools of biology differ on how humans acquired speech but agree that the synapsid—a common reptile ancestor we share with other mammals—had the first ear bone that resonated sounds to its brain. Synapsids roamed this planet more than two hundred million years ago.)

Whence cometh our language?

The Bible makes no mention of from whence came such a wondrous gift.

Believers in intelligent design contend that the power of speech evolved through a process too complex to have taken place without God's guidance.

Most evolutionists favor Savannah theory

In the early 1930s, when I was growing up, most public school textbooks cited the evolutionists' Savannah theory, believing that our apelike ancestors did the following:

- Moved out of the forests onto Africa's grassy plains (savannahs).
- Learned to stand upright so they could look over the tall prairie grasses to sight both predators and prey and throw a spear.
- Freed their hands for tools and fire by walking upright.
- Developed language by acquiring sweat glands so that they no longer panted in the heat.
- Sweat so much chasing after prey in the sunny savannahs that they lost their body hair.

Long umbilical cords an aquatic legacy?

Did the flooding of the Red Sea about five million years ago separate our ancestors from other primates and force them to live in flooded, swampy areas?

Based on a theory developed in 1930 by British marine biologist Alistair Hardy, Elaine Morgan's provocative book *Aquatic Apes* suggests such a scenario.

Many anthropologists remain skeptical of Morgan's Aquatic Apes theory, but to me a number of her conclusions seem far more logical than most of those in the savannah theory.

Human babies, unlike ape babies, can swim at birth. One of Morgan's more intriguing rationales suggests that aquatic ape babies' long umbilical cords might have allowed them to be born underwater, swim to the surface, and grab on to the mother's hair. (Hair roots, she says, strengthen during pregnancy.)

Did changes let throat, tongue, and lips harmonize?

Biologist Hardy contended that primates—forced from the forest by competition—moved to the seashore to search for food. There, they learned to become bipedal by keeping their heads above the water while they let the water support their weight.

Body changes that let us walk upright did free our hands for tools and fire, but changes in our throat, tongue, and lips probably created a much more significant advantage.

Morgan and her backers contend that our ancestors probably didn't master language until they emerged from an aquatic era after having acquired:

- A thick layer of blubber that we call subcutaneous fat not found on other apes but also found on aquatic mammals, such as whales, dolphins, and seals.
- Our lack of body hair—again similar to aquatic animals.
- Greasy waterproofing skin.
- Very tiny webbing between the fingers.
- Voluntary breath control, such as the kind marine mammals and birds possess.
- A hooded nose with nostrils pointed downward.
- A body streamlined for swimming.
- Ability to swim even as babies.
- Bipedal stance perpendicular.

Drop of the larynx key to our speech

Perhaps the most significant aquatic-era change in our ancestors was the position of the larynx.

Our larynx is that lump we call our "Adam's apple."

Most mammals' larynxes sit upright behind the tongue and in the back of the nose. With the larynx in that position, most of the exhaled air passes out through the nostrils, resulting in mostly nasal sounds.

When we talk, on the other hand, most of the air goes out through our mouths, not our noses. We exhale through the nose to make only a few sounds, such as nasal consonants like "m" or "n."

Lowering the larynx improved the quality of our vowels and made speech easier to understand.

Our windpipe opening, however, sits squarely in the path of descending food, where it makes it easier for us to choke to death if a chunk of meat goes down the wrong way. That's something that rarely happens to a dog or a cat.

Did shellfish nourish our brains?

One other intriguing "water monkey" concept cites "evidence that the large brains of the earliest humans probably evolved from their nutrient-rich shoreline diet."

In 2009, Charles Weatherby wrote in *Vital Choices*, an online newsletter: "More recent research indicates that some early human ancestors lived on the seacoast of East Africa and ate easy-to-harvest shellfish—like today's scallops—in abundance."

Renowned British brain researcher Michael Crawford, PhD, argues quite persuasively that humans could not have developed such disproportionately big brains without having lived primarily on aquatic animals and plants from shallow fresh and coastal waters.

Dr. Crawford also notes that the famed prehistoric female, "Lucy," was discovered at the Olduvai Gorge. When Lucy and her clan lived there, that gorge was the Olduvai River.

Agree with Dr. Crawford or not, but it's easy to admire the creativity of his reasoning that our species—having lived in watery swamps in East Africa for millions of years—spawned a deep-seated penchant of vacationers around the globe to head for the beaches.

Brain, our hard drive; neurons, its circuits

The brain is our system's hard drive; neurons, its circuits.

Our mouths handle the output; our ears, the input.

The operating system's software lets us build intricate, comprehensible words and phrases.

By controlling the breath we exhale, we communicate precise thoughts from person to person.

Human life in its present form would be impossible and inconceivable without the gift of language. Living organisms all die, but oral or written language lets the human mind—to some degree—survive past death.

Since our very beginnings, language has been the characteristic that defines us. It's the basis of human cooperation.

We Homo sapiens outlive our life spans by sounding symbols to educate our offspring. We share our knowledge with them. They, in turn, similarly pass that knowledge on from generation to generation via sound symbols.

Our fully articulated language of sound symbols allowed our ancestors to share knowledge that gave our species the powers needed to dominate this planet.

Spoken sound symbols—whether a gift from God or evolutionary— still underpin all information technology.

Adam's Apple
vital role as
Information Technology[3]

The Bible tells us that Eve gave Adam fruit from the Tree of Knowledge of Good and Evil, and Adam bit into it. What the fruit was, the Bible doesn't say, but legend calls it an apple and tells us that Adam—frightened by God's approaching footsteps—gulped it down so fast that it stuck in his throat.

So the lump in the your neck became your "Adam's apple."

Larynx is the anatomical term for that lump of cartilage that forms the front wall of the human voice box. Two vocal cords attached to it run along the inside edge of two tiny folds of skin. When you engage them to vocalize, they stretch across the windpipe.

Our epiglottis, a thin flap of flexible tissue attached to the top of the voice box, is unique to humans. When we swallow, it folds back to block entry of food into the windpipe. Otherwise that flap stays open and allows the air that powers our sound system to pass through.

Most other animals' voice boxes sit upright behind the tongue and into the back of the nose, and most of the exhaled air passes out through the nostrils. That produces mostly nasal sounds.

Human voice boxes sit lower in the throat. When we talk, most of the air passes out through our mouths, not our noses.

We exhale through the nose to make only a few sounds, such as nasal consonants like "m" or "n."

Lowering the voice box made speech easier to understand.

Even in these digital times, Adam's apples continue to expand the sharing of what must be the ultimate fruit from the Tree of Knowledge of Good and Evil.

Few tales are better known, but some readers may have been as surprised as I to learn that the Adam's apple frames a major piece vital to Homo sapiens first information technology.

---

3   Search Wikipedia for "Larynx" AND Google images for "Adam's apple"

CHAPTER 2

For millennia, memory reigned over commerce, news,
craft skills, and entertainment. It also garnered,
preserved, and stored the fruits of education.
—Daniel J. Boorstin (1914-2004)

The Gift of Memory

With our wondrous speech hardware and software came another hardware gift—our brain's memory. To exchange information, our earliest ancestors whispered, spoke, shouted, beat drums, and sent smoke signals.

Sounds and their echoes vanish into the air, as does smoke. So the accuracy of any later transmission rested solely upon the memory of those who heard the original words.

Mnemonics' enormous possibilities

Octogenarians like myself decry episodic "senior moments" of forgetfulness, but few of us ever took full advantage of our species' remarkable mnemonic capabilities.

In *The Discoverers*, his sweeping history of man's search to know himself, Daniel J. Boorstin writes that memory "ruled daily life" before the printed book and fully deserved to be labeled the "art preservative of all arts."

For millennia, memory presided over commerce, craft skills, news, and entertainment. It also garnered, preserved, and stored the fruits of education.

Troubadours—people able to repeat a thousand words after hearing them just once—delivered most news from the outside world that didn't come through the church.

Rhyming verses provided the key to memory in that oral world.

Even the courts were oral, so judges had to store the laws in their memories. The young looked up to the old, who held captured history in their memories.

Boorstin relates awesome mnemonic skills that bloomed in ancient times. Take, for instance, the legendary Greek lyric poet Simonides of Ceos, credited with having invented the mnemonic art in the sixth century BC.

Simonides formalized his memory system and made it available for others to imitate. He instructed his pupils to select places and then form mental images in them.

That way the order of the places might preserve the order of the bits to be memorized. Similar memory skills kept Western epics alive for centuries.

Students warehoused memory

To perpetuate classics, such as the *Iliad* and the *Odyssey*, troubadours filled memorized lists of spaces with visual details to bring to mind thousands of lines of poetry. Church ritual and liturgy were passed down in the same manner.

A report from the Middle Ages tells of seeing students of rhetoric in that era "walking tensely through a deserted building (often a temple or a chapel) noting the shape and furnishing of each room to equip his imagination with places to warehouse his memory."

The accuracy of our ancient forbearers' spoken messages rested solely upon the listener's memory.

CHAPTER 3

*Did a wall of seawater first seep and then surge from
the Mediterranean into the huge depression
we know today as the Black Sea?*

Whence Cometh Indo-European Tongues?

In prehistoric times—antedating written history by millennia—a large freshwater lake lay halfway between the English Channel and today's boundary between Pakistan and India.

A thriving agrarian civilization with a common language had evolved around the lake's sandy shores. Hundreds of miles from the nearest seashore, its people probably had no idea that melting of the last ice age had been lifting sea levels very gradually for several thousand years.

A wall of seawater first seeped and then surged from the Mediterranean into the huge depression known today as the Black Sea.

Driven from their homes by that fearsome flood, survivors dispersed to the four winds.

By the fifteenth century, their descendants had spread as far north as the seashore above Scandinavia, as far west as the Atlantic Ocean, as far northeast as the Pacific, and as far southeast as India.

As they dispersed, generation after generation scattered seeds of their unique language. Those seeds took root and eventually grafted onto the languages of the lands in which they sprouted.

Salt sea buried freshwater sands

That process may have spawned the Indo-European family of languages, but lacking the power of the written word, nobody from that era has left us proof one way or another.

This Black Sea-genesis account dovetails with conclusions outlined in *Noah's Flood,* a book written by marine geologists William Ryan and Walter Pitman and published in 1998. Freshwater sands were discovered later on the salt sea's bottom by *National Geographic* expeditions led by Robert Ballard, famed for his recovery of the sunken Titanic.

Many scholars dispute the *Noah's Flood* account, but it seems consistent with the generally accepted theses that the Indo-European language family (1) evolved from one aboriginal ancestral tongue and (2) split geographically along a line that runs roughly from Scandinavia to Greece and almost touches the Black Sea.

The eastward migration from the Black Sea left tongue-prints in Albanian, Armenian, Balto-Slavic, Indian, and Iranian branches.

To the west, Celtic, Hellenic, Italic, and Teutonic sibling tongues emerged.

Noah's Flood's
language impact [4]

Did members of an agrarian community on the northeast shores of a freshwater lake flee from a flood of Mediterranean seawater, scatter in all directions and seed the tongues of today's speakers of Indo-European languages?

A line in map connecting the Baltic Sea and India seems to demark halfway between the ends of the then-known world where those languages had spread—perhaps in just such a scenario.

---

4   Search Wikipedia for "Black Sea Deluge Theory" and Google images for "black sea" and "indo-european"

CHAPTER 4

Before the advent of literacy, the distance a man could ride a horse in one day marked the physical limit of a kingdom. A king could impose his will on his troops and people only that far.

Scripting Symbols of Shape

Our ancestors survived on planet Earth for half a million years, unable to communicate beyond the reach of their voices, drums, or smoke signals.

They depended for the most part upon spoken sound symbols to share information that they stored in their memories.

When they created agrarian economies, however, they needed a better information technology to augment memories that resided in the brain's technology.

Prehistoric nomadic herding, hunting, and gathering societies had, of course, devised primitive, nonverbal mnemonic methods.

They used crude tools, such as sticks, rock, and bone, to draw pictures on the walls of caves. They also notched sticks or knotted strings to help keep track of the days, weeks, and years. Cave carvings passed down stories to future generations with images of hunts and battles.

Other ways to expand memory included textile patterns that tell stories. Consider the legend of Philomela:

Rape victim weaves her revenge

King Tereus of Thrace agreed to travel to Athens and escort his wife Procne's sister, Philomela, to Thrace for a visit. Tereus lusted for Philomela on the voyage. When they arrived in Thrace, he forced her to a cabin in the woods and raped her.

The defiant Philomela proclaimed to her rapist that now she had no shame and, if given the chance, she'd "tell everybody."

Tereus's response was to cut out her tongue and leave her in the cabin. There, Philomela wove a tapestry that told her story and had it sent to Procne.

Her sister's sordid textile tale so infuriated Procne that she killed her son by Tereus. Then she served his son to his father, who unknowingly ate him. When he discovered what had been done, Tereus tried to kill both sisters. They fled, and he pursued. In the end, the Olympic gods changed all three into birds.

Cave drawings, notched sticks, tapestries, and the like, however, marked but baby steps beyond the limitations of our first information technology.

Mnemonics skills that once worked well for poet-singers' stories failed to meet the needs of an economic species that irrigated fields, planted crops, and raised livestock.

With growing awareness of the idea of property—now in the form of land, labor, and commodities—came trade and the need to keep accounts.

Judicial systems built upon oral decrees rested upon shaky mnemonic foundations.

InfoTech through time and space

In about 3500 BC, many nomadic tribes—rather than migrate seasonally—settled down in southern Mesopotamia to pioneer year-round agriculture.

There between the rivers of the Tigris and Euphrates, they developed an Information Technology that laid the foundation for probably the earliest civilization on earth.

Prehistoric herders, gatherers, and hunters who abandoned the nomadic life soon learned that their memories could not handle the recordkeeping agrarian societies demanded. So they translated spoken words into symbol-shape writing systems.

In the beginning, symbols, such as those of animals and farm commodities, inscribed on tokens transmitted knowledge through both time and space. Then, primarily to register accounts, Sumerian scribes wrote similar symbols on clay tablets in script known as cuneiform (*cuneus*: wedge; *form*: shaped).

This pioneer writing system then arranged the same token figures not just to manage accounts but also to convey messages and accommodate literature.

The written word spoke through time and space to unlimited numbers of persons, not just to those within earshot who might repeat what people said.

Writing gradually replaced the mnemonics of past civilizations.
Being able to write and read shape symbols made it possible to accumulate and share far more knowledge than any one person might memorize in a lifetime. Writing also let successive generations of observers check, recheck, and update the accuracy of reports.

Warrior-rulers now could command troops well beyond the boundaries formerly limited by the distance a horse could carry a man in one day and gain control over regions large enough to grow into the world's first city-states.

Temples, such as those in Ur, Babylon, and Nineveh, towered over walled fortresses surrounded by villages, hamlets, and irrigated fields. They served as the religious, governmental, educational, and commercial centers of their age.

As temple complexes grew into major economic enterprises, many workers were needed to handle large quantities of goods.

Royalty and temple priests used the then-revolutionary InfoTech to record sales of land, crops, and livestock, not to mention taxes, payrolls, and tributes.

Clay tablets the most enduring records
Sumerian scribes pressed the triangular tip of a stylus into soft clay tablets to inscribe wedge-shaped pictographs. Each character represented a word or syllable according to the position in which it pointed. The tablets were then dried in the sun or fired in ovens.

Millions of surviving tablets establish that etched clay endures as history's most lasting form of recordkeeping.

Over centuries, Mesopotamian scribes improved script capabilities so that even men separated by hundreds of miles could exchange their thoughts with infinitely more clarity than had been the case five centuries earlier.

By about 1800 BC, Babylon's King Hammurabi (d. 1750 BC) had seized upon script's expanded word powers.

They let his administration scatter soldiers to points far from his person and summon them for service when needed. After he conquered all the city-states in Mesopotamia, the king initiated a series of reforms to pave the way for a "Golden Age of Babylon."

Hammurabi took advantage of his scribes' ability to convert ordinary speech into pictograph symbols easily translated throughout his kingdom. He dictated royal laws to his scribes that provided uniform justice for all the Babylonian city-states and covered many aspects of daily life.

Records of landholding rights, obligations toward individuals, judicial decisions, and administrative instructions all served to give coherence and scope to governmental actions across space and time.

Other shape-symbol systems developed elsewhere

While writing with cuneiform continued under development in Mesopotamia, other pictograph systems began appearing in India and as far away as China.

In nearby Egypt, hieroglyphics were used more to record religious dogma and to glorify and proclaim the supremacy of the Egyptian king than for recordkeeping.

Mesopotamia, Egypt, India, and China, the major pioneer agrarian civilizations on planet Earth, all developed their pictographic languages independently, as did the Mayans in southern Mexico and Guatemala.

As noted previously, all those languages scripted symbols for words or syllables. Some read from left to right, others right to left or from top to bottom or back and forth like the rows in a plowed field.

Scribe-clerks underwent rigorous training

Originally the province of priests, recordkeeping expanded, and clerks were trained for scribal duties.

In the Louvre sits a stone statue of *the Scribe Squatting on His Haunches.* He's almost totally nude, with a pen behind his ear—besides the one he wields.

To qualify for his job, a scribe had to undergo a rigorous training period that included dictation and copying, reading, and chanting in unison.

Whether pictographic, logographic (symbols representing whole words), or syllabic, each system required its scribes to memorize hundreds, if not thousands of symbols.

Charting stars empowered temple priests

Priests in those towering temples able to read, write, add, and subtract dazzled their audience.

In his provocative book, *Zero: The Biography of a Dangerous Idea,* Charles Seife writes that Mesopotamian priests ranked just below warrior-kings and courts in the royal hierarchy.

Seife suggests that these scribe-mathematicians probably gained control of the temple warehouses by being able to record the passage of celestial events, date annual river floods, and time the planting of seeds.

With their warrior-rulers, they became an elite group with enormous powers over a huge illiterate minority and tended to restrict the sharing of problem-solving knowledge.

The magic of writing broke ancient tribal bonds and passed the tribal chiefs' powers to warrior-leaders and priests more inclined to wield than to share the power of knowledge this wondrous Information Technology bestowed upon them.

We'll see ahead how most later InfoTech revolutions contrarily distributed power and wealth to a growing literate populace.

CHAPTER 5

The alphabet made the pen mightier than the sword.
It generated powers of knowledge greater than
the powers of kings' marching warriors.

Symbols-of-Sound Demand Analysis

To Abe Lincoln, the alphabet was "the world's greatest invention."

What made the switch from pictographic writing's shape symbols to the phonetic alphabet's sound symbols so great?

The twenty-six letters of our alphabet are without doubt much easier to master than hundreds of pictographs. In addition, the alphabet freed scribes from spending most of their time dealing with pictograph script's growing complexities

Nevertheless, the alphabet rises to true greatness mostly because it gives us an eye for an ear.

It forces us to match each letter with a sound and vice versa. Meaningless alphabetic symbols correspond with otherwise meaningless sounds.

In order to form any word, one must:
- Analyze its phonic structure,
- Break it down into its basic sounds, and then
- Match letters with the phonic elements to spell it.

Forming spoken words from letters this way introduced a revolutionary thinking process. Adding one sound after another, as in c-a-t, becomes very simple and natural. Simple as this system may seem, it's one of the most ingenious ever devised by man.

In his illuminating book *The Alphabet Effect*, Robert K. Logan notes that every time a word is written, we repeat this sequential analysis or linear thinking.

That, he claims, sublimely promotes the skills of analysis and matching that are so critical to developing logical, mathematical, and scientific thinking.

How phonetic writing came into being

Pictographic script, the first writing system to communicate through space and time, reigned for millennia as the ancient world's premier Information Technology.

As that writing system aged, however, it became increasingly abstract. The more abstract it became, the more challenging the learning process became. One had to memorize so many symbols that it took twelve years of schooling just to learn to read, write, and do simple arithmetic.

Pictographic culture's rigorous nature, moreover, left priests and scribes with little time or motivation for creativity.

Phoenicians, Egyptians, Assyrians, and Hebrews intermingled along the Mediterranean's eastern shores for the four centuries before 1500 BC. Bringing together those different cultures must have made it obvious that they needed an easier way to communicate.

In any case, creative Semitic-speaking scribes took centuries to develop the system that replaced symbols of shape with the alphabet's symbols of sound.

For millennia, most historians tended to credit the Phoenicians with inventing the first phonetic alphabet. In 1999, however, Egyptologists said they traced each of our alphabet's twenty-six letters back to Egyptian hieroglyphic symbols—often even to the same sound value it had eight thousand years ago.

Phoenician ABCs lineage survives

Whether innovators in Phoenicia or in Egypt adopted the first alphabet, Phoenicia became the first state-level society to make extensive use of a sound-symbol alphabet, and only alphabetic offspring of phonetic Phoenician lineage prevail to this day.

Phoenicians were much more powerful than the Hebrews during the reign of King Hiram (1000–947 BC), the monarch who sold the cedars to

King Solomon (1011–931 BC). Their homeland lay along the coastal regions known today as Israel, Lebanon, Syria, and the Palestinian Territories.

The Greeks named them "phonics" (the purple people) in recognition of the precious purple "Tyrian" cloth they produced. Shipped from Tyre, their main port and trading center, it was extremely costly and was worn as mark of imperial or royal rank.

Phoenicians were seafaring traders using manpowered sailing galleys. They transported goods all across the Mediterranean and even on into the Atlantic Ocean.

Sailing out from their homeland, they established trading centers and gradually spread their alphabet's use to places as far-flung as Greece, Sicily, Italy, North Africa, southern Spain, and the British Isles.

Vowel signs were missing

The Phoenician's twenty-two signs caused ambiguities, so the Greeks converted vowel-related signs from Hebrew and other Semitic systems to create the vowels that made the Greek alphabet the most accurate and unambiguous phonetic system known to man. It combines unique visual signs into unique arrays. These form unique spoken words that create a one-to-one correspondence between the written and the spoken language.

The Greek alphabet's twenty-six letters [5] seem minuscule when compared to the thousand basic Chinese characters or the hundreds of hieroglyphs or cuneiform signs.

ABCs function as organizing tool

Compared to pictographic systems, the alphabet makes it much easier to store and retrieve data.

By organizing entries alphabetically, dictionaries, encyclopedias, and library catalogs let us go quickly to a section with entries beginning with any one of the twenty-six letters from A to Z. Once we know our ABCs, this is a simple, easily mastered procedure.

---

5   Alphabets come in different sizes and styles; one example, the fourteen-letter Hawaiian system.

Similarly, business offices use it to file and retrieve their written materials.

I have to admit to complete ignorance about how pictographic material might be catalogued, but the thought of dealing with thousands or even just hundreds of characters seems overwhelming. How would pictographic material be catalogued? The thought of dealing with thousands—or just hundreds—of characters is overwhelming.

The alphabet made the pen mightier than the sword.

It coupled its expanded power of sharing knowledge with its linear power of analytical thinking to surpass the powers of monarchies and their marching warriors.

(Had monopoly of the privileged scribe-mathematician cliques remained in place, who would have scripted the angry words of those biblical prophets who so freely attacked established practices?)

It's quite ironic, however, that:

- The alphabet's rigid logic helped hide the dangerous but vital missing number, which Chapter 11 shall try to rescue from obscurity, and that forced a detour to the East before modern science could develop.
- Teaching children the alphabet today—their first step to literacy— takes place totally in the oral mode, and the Phoenicians who fathered its birth left very few remains of their writings.

I'm convinced that the alphabet was *an* agent (again agreeing with Eisenstein's thinking) but not necessarily *the* agent that generated powers of problem-solving knowledge needed to build and govern empires.

To me, it's only logical that increased access to problem-solving knowledge must have played a vital role in the empire building by Alexander the Great, but his empire did not long survive his early death.

The Golden Alphabet Age

Passed on to the Etruscans and Romans, the enormously enriched Greek alphabet fueled Rome's golden alphabet age with shared powers of knowledge sufficient to keep it virile for five hundred years—from the days of Pericles to the beginning of the decline of the Roman Empire.

In 2011 the United States is less than half that age.

CHAPTER 6

*"Chinese ships had reached America seventy years before Columbus
and a century before Magellan circumnavigated the globe."*
—History hobbyist Gavin Menzies (1937–)

China's InfoTech Siblings

After Christ's ministry, Western Civilization slid into the shadows of what some call the Dark Ages. Meanwhile two historic Information Technologies—paper and print—were lifting China toward new heights.

Insects had kept paper a secret from our ancestors for about a million years, including the first four thousand years after writing's invention. In addition to clay, papyrus, and parchment, other writing surfaces before the invention of paper included leaves from palm and olive trees and the bark of trees.

Papyrus, an expensive but superior writing surface

Pressing triangular-tipped styluses into soft moist clay had to be messy and cumbersome. Papyrus offered a much better writing surface, but it was more expensive to produce.

Workers had to harvest papyrus reeds from marshes in the River Nile, strip them of their hard outer fibers, and then slice the core into short strips. After they soaked them in water, they would:

- Pound the strips nearly dry before overlapping them slightly.
- Place a second set of strips at right angles to the first.
- Pound those sheets and leave them to dry under a heavy weight.

They pasted manuscript sheets together, attached a wooden rod to each end, and rolled the long piece onto the right rod.

A scribe unrolled a few inches of the scroll to open each column of writing surface. To return to the start of the scroll, this process was reversed.

Rolling and unrolling the scrolls—some ran to 150 papyrus pages—was a nuisance.

Even so, papyrus was so far superior to clay tablets—or bark or leaves—that Egypt eventually banned papyrus exports to protect its Ptolemy[6] rulers' reputation as the greatest patrons of science and scholarship.

Parchment challenges Egypt's papyrus

More than a century before Christ, King Eumenes II of Pergamum built a library to compete with Egypt's Alexandria Library. Unable to find another comparable source of papyrus, Pergamum turned to parchment.

Parchment was expensive, but had several advantages:

- It was longer lasting.
- Its surface was smoother.
- One could write on both its back and front.
- It did not crack when folded.
- When folded, it could be sewn together to make a codex, precursor of the books we know today.

One Bible took a hundred young animals' hides

To make parchment, sheep or goat hides are scraped clean to remove the hairs. Then the hides were rubbed smooth with pumice; washed and dressed with chalk; and finished with a lime-based wash.

Vellum—the highest grade of parchment—was made of the skin of stillborn or very young animals. It was preferred for its suppleness, thinness, and absence of imperfections, but it took the almost a hundred hides to produce one vellum Bible.

---

6   An intriguing research discovery was finding that Cleopatra's lineage was Greek, not Egyptian. Ptolemy I, her dynasty's pharaoh, was Alexander the Great's boyhood friend.

Parchment was still often preferred to paper in the transitional era when decorative miniatures and illumination embellished manuscripts. [7]

Even today, it is used for certain documents and diplomas, for book bindings and lampshades, and for the heads of drums, tambourines, and banjos.

Chinese writing serves multiple tongues

Chinese reigns as the oldest written language in continuous use since the time of its invention.

Royal Chinese priests, according to the Oriental Institute's Christopher Woods, invented that language's symbols to write out questions they wanted the gods to answer.

The questions were written on ox bones or the tummies of turtle shells, which were heated in fires until they cracked. From the way they cracked, the priests supposed they could divine the answers.

Most words in ancient China could be spoken with a single syllable, so it's logical that the written language is logographic (i.e., each character represents a single word or syllable).

(Our English is mainly a language of sound symbols, but we readily recognize logograms such as the ampersand and the dollar sign.)

In Chinese, some characters represent same-sounding syllables with different meanings.

To become literate in Chinese, one must memorize thousands of syllables rather than just the few dozen letters needed for phonetic alphabets. Despite regional and cultural differences in everyday speech, literate Chinese all read and write the same script.

The Chinese language's continuity and flexibility has sustained China's culture down through the ages—perhaps most significantly by helping to unify China's diverse ethnic groups.

"Classic Chinese," first written on silk cloth or sheets of bamboo strips, appeared sometime between one and two millennia after cuneiform

---

7   In the early days of printing, many decried the absence of such decorative embellishments in printed books.

and hieroglyphics. It has survived despite numerous episodic attempts to displace it.

Papermaking a long-kept secret

An insect we relate more to its sting than to its engineering skills now flies into this InfoTech tale's nest.

Paper wasps have been making a paste that dries as paper for eons by chewing tiny slivers of wood..

T'sai Lun, a scholarly Chinese official, watched closely as wasps separated plant fibers, suspended them in water, and let them dry into woven mats of paper.

After he ground up hemp, old cloth, and mulberry bark, mixed them with water, and pounded them with a wooden tool, he poured the mixture onto a flat piece of coarsely woven cloth and let the water drain through. That left only the fibers on the cloth.

Once they had dried, he saw that he had created a flexible, lightweight sheet of quality writing surface. (The process is so elegantly simple that anyone can recreate it at home.)

T'sai Lun recorded his invention in 105 AD.

Chinese appear to have first used coarsely woven cloth stretched inside a bamboo frame as a sieve to dip the fiber slurry from a vat and hold it for drying, but later, they developed a smooth material for the mold covering that could be reused immediately.

Stealing the wasp's secret enabled China to substitute paper for silk. That freed its silk industry to increase profits from the silk trade by concentrating on producing the cloth fabric.

Following the lead of the wasps, the Chinese kept papermaking a secret for centuries—until the Battle of Talas in 751 in Central Asia.

Paper superior in many ways

Paper offers many advantages over other writing surfaces:

- It's easy to write on with many plentiful common tools like ink pens or brushes, pencils, crayons, and paints.

- Its length, width, weight, and quality can readily be controlled, while its light weight makes easily transportable.
- As a medium of exchange, paper money, moreover, frees precious metals, such as gold and silver, for productive purposes that yield higher income.

(Professor Hart points out that paper's low cost made it possible for libraries not only to afford to stack more books but also to produce inexpensive indexes and catalogs that made the books' contents more accessible.)

Block printing vs. movable type

The second Chinese InfoTech sibling was print.

Historian Jared Diamond decries the popular belief in the Western world that printing began with Johann Gutenberg in 1454. By then, Diamond notes, wood-block printing had been practiced in China for centuries. Koreans, moreover, had successfully printed with movable type, but the hundreds of letters in the Korean script made it impractical.

The key to the success of the Gutenberg Press—and to its astonishing immediate impact—would be its marriage to the West's phonetic languages with the twenty-six-letter alphabet—as opposed to logographic writing's thousands of symbols.

Asian histories emphasize that development of wood-block printing led to the rise in China of a highly literate society sharing the power of knowledge centuries before one arose in Europe.

The Chinese had already quite refined the block printing process as early as the seventh century, but most historians concede that Feng Tao (882–954) was the "Eastern Father of Printing."

The wood-block technique advanced rapidly. By 1000, paged books in the modern style had replaced scrolls. Two-color printing (black and red) was seen as early as 1340.

Marco Polo hailed literate China's wonders

The journeys of Marco Polo (1254–1324) through Asia lasted twenty-four years. His travelogue featured cities with golden roofs in a Chinese culture so far superior to anything in the West that it dazzled his readers.

Besides flourishing in the arts, society, and social life, China also boasted:

- Paper currency.
- An efficient postal system.
- The Great Wall that stretched farther than from New York to Los Angeles.
- The 1,103-mile Grand Canal 's locks could lift boats up into land more than 150 feet above sea level.

Detailed accounts support the gist of Marco Polo's fourteenth-century tales of wealthy Chinese city-states with populations in the millions that far outshone even leading trading centers in Europe. Nevertheless, I find no Western scholars linking that awakening to the problem-solving knowledge power that China's InfoTech siblings must have generated.

Marco Polo touted
China's magnificence [8]

The Chinese Imperial Palace wasn't built until almost a century after the death of Marco Polo, but it typified the magnificence of the China Polo visited.

Detailed accounts support the gist of Polo's fourteenth-century tales of wealthy Chinese city-states with populations in the millions that far outshone even leading trading centers in Europe. Yet I find no Western scholars linking that awakening to the problem-solving knowledge power generated by China's InfoTech siblings.

According to the son of Christopher Columbus, Polo's epic travelogue aroused his father's interest in the possibility of finding an oceanic Silk Road to China and its riches.

8   Search Wikipedia for "Marco Polo" and Google images for "Chinese Imperial Palace"

CHAPTER 7

The Koran teaches that the human world's
quest for knowledge leads to further
knowing of Allah.

Islam's Great Gifts to the West

Little more than a century after the death of Muhammad (c570–632), Allah and the laws of Islam held sway:

- From Arabia across northern Africa to Spain.
- Throughout most of the Middle East.
- Across Central Asia as far east as the Punjab on the India-Pakistan border.

For more than three decades, the Arabs had been in control of Samarkand—a wealthy Central Asia trading station where the silks of China were exchanged for the fabrics of Persia.

For more than seven centuries, the Chinese had managed to keep control of their secret of papermaking, but the arrogance of one of T'ang Emperor Hsuan-tsung's generals opened the way near Samarkand for the secret's escape.

After the arrogant Chinese general completed his emperor's assignment to clear a Tibetan blockade of the East-West trade route, he proceeded on his own volition to Tashkent, a prosperous neighbor city-state 175 miles northeast of Samarkand.

The general presented a list of demands to the Tashnet king, a Turk who was an acknowledged subject of China. Because the general thought the Turk's answers to his demands were impertinent, he had the king beheaded.

The dead king's son appealed to Samarkand. When its Arab Caliphate agreed to take the former prince's side in his dispute with China, the stage was for a pivotal clash between Arab and Chinese forces.

In the summer of 751 AD, the Arab forces ended China's Central Asia adventure by routing the T'ang Dynasty's Army in the historic five-day Battle of Talas.

Arabs capture Chinese papermakers

In their flight along the crowded, rough, and rugged road toward the eastern mountains, Chinese soldiers died by the thousands, but the Arabs singled out from among the fleeing refugees a number of Chinese papermakers. Taken prisoner and led back to Samarkand, these skilled craftsmen were put to work building the first paper mill outside of China's control.

From Samarkand, the Islamic paper trail crept slowly westward. Muslim freebooters conquered Crete and invaded Sicily in the ninth century.

Cairo was making paper by the tenth century; then it was on to Tunisia and Islamic Spain by the eleventh.

Papermaking reached Italy by way of Sicily in 1268, but Central Europe didn't take up paper until the fourteenth century.

Both Hebrew and Islamic scripture had been written on parchment, and both religions hesitated to put scripture on anything so modest as paper despite its strength and durability. Similarly, some Christians called it an infidel technology and slowed the flow of paper into Europe.

Islamic Golden Age takes root

Under Koran's teachings, however, Muslim scholars furthered the knowing of Allah by continuing research and experiments. Access to cheaper and more plentiful supplies of writing surfaces after the Battle of Talas eventually made it far easier them to carry out that mandate.

Under Abbasid caliphs, the Islamic Golden Age took root in the ninth century, and—until the Mongols sacked Baghdad in 1256—the splendor and learning of Muslim culture was unparalleled.

Extensive ancient Greek and Roman teachings formed the foundation of the classical tradition, but most of it had been lost in the wake of the internal collapse of the Roman Empire and ongoing barbarian invasions. For example, most of Aristotle's books had been unavailable in Europe for centuries.

After the Battle of Talas, Muslim scholars flocked to Baghdad, where availability of inexpensive paper let them copy Greek and Persian writings and introduce science into the Arab world. Many of the *Thousand and One Night Tales* are set in Baghdad during this period.

Islamic gathering of knowledge then moved west along the path of papermaking, finally concentrating in Spain in the twelfth and thirteenth centuries. With a population then of about a half million—more than thirteen times that of Paris—Cordoba was on its way to succeed Constantinople as the largest and most prosperous city in Europe.

Islam's "Golden Age" saved much Greek, Egyptian, and Roman learning from being lost forever. Only by using Islamic translations of the Greek's writings would European philosophers rediscover them.

Islam also brought to Europe the compass—another Chinese trophy from the Battle of Talas. It proved indispensable as a navigation tool for ocean explorers in the fifteenth and sixteenth centuries.

Absent those factors, it's difficult to imagine Europe's Renaissance rising to the heights it reached.

The InfoTech trail detours to northeast Asia

Ahead lies the tale of an information technology—the "nothing number" so enormously significant to modern science. It lay undiscovered for ages in Babylon just as the paper secret avoided notice for eons in wasps' nests.

Now, however, the InfoTech trail jumps to Western Europe before heading for the far reaches of northeast Asia.

West's debt to Islamic warriors and scholars [9]

After the Battle of Talas in 751 robbed China of its papermaking secret, Arab conquests continued across northern Africa to Spain, throughout most of the Middle East, and across Central Asia as far east as the Punjab on the India-Pakistan border.

The Koran teaches that the human world's quest for knowledge leads to further knowing of Allah. Islamic scholars milked the classic tradition in Babylon, moved west along the path of papermaking, and finally concentrated in Spain. Cordoba's population swelled to about a half million—more than thirteen times that of Paris—and the city would succeed Constantinople as the largest and most prosperous city in Europe.

Islam's "Golden Age" saved much Greek, Egyptian, and Roman learning from being lost forever. Islam also passed on China's wasp-paper secret that gave the West access to a much less costly writing surface.

---

9   Search Google Images for "Abbasids dynasty" and Wikipedia for "Koran"

CHAPTER 8

*The Carolingian dynasty was named for Charles Martel,
Charlemagne's grandfather, who halted the Muslim
Army's advance across the Pyrenees in 732.*

Charlemagne and Medieval Europe

The Arabs were still in the early stages of their conquests when a warrior-king in France hired a cleric educator from York, England, who would develop a significant information technology. Together, they launched a mini-renaissance about five centuries before the start of the Italian Renaissance.

The cleric was a scholarly monk named Alcuin.

The warrior-king was Charlemagne—in Latin, Carlos Magnus (742–814). He was of the Carolingian dynasty that controlled France from the eighth through the tenth centuries and was crowned the first ruler of the Holy Roman Empire in 800.

Before recalling their accomplishments, let's look to the times in which they are set.

The medieval period (or Middle Ages) began about 500 AD with the fall of the Roman Empire and lasted about a thousand years.

Western Europe's economy deteriorated drastically after the breakdown of law and order in the first half of this period. The resulting unstable environment for trade, business, and industry destabilized the rest of civilization as well.

All education declined drastically—from the lowest level to the highest. Literacy rates plummeted. Legend and myth tended to compete with hard-earned knowledge. Many modern historians decry the idea that conditions were so bad that progress stopped altogether for half a millennium, but the recovery during those "Dark Ages" was very sluggish.

Setting the stage for Gutenberg

One truly historic invention—or imported innovation—stands out, however, among the few advances.

In his lucid history of *The Rise of the West*, William H. McNeill points to the huge impact the introduction of the moldboard plow exerted on Europe's economy.

Those heavy metal plows turned over furrows to create artificial ridges and hollows in even the flattest fields. That drained surplus water from lands otherwise unusable and readied the soil for planting sooner by drastically cutting the time needed to plow a field.

It took from the sixth to the tenth century for this type of plow to become established in Europe, partly because it was only effective on large fields and needed a team of four or more oxen to pull it. In addition, the intellectual lethargy of the period slowed the rapid spread of new ideas.

New planting system adopted

More protein-filled legumes were added to the European diet after the ninth century when farmers in Europe started replacing a two-field crop rotation with a three-field rotation.

Under two-field rotation, half the land had been planted in a year while the other half lay fallow. In the next year, the two fields were reversed.

Under three-field rotation, the land was divided into three parts: In the fall, one section was planted with winter wheat or rye. In spring, the second field was planted with other crops such as peas, lentils, or beans. The third field was left unplanted to rest.

Under the two-field system with six hundred acres of fertile land, one field was planted and the other left fallow so only three hundred acres were harvested.

On the same acreage under the three-field system, the spring crops were mostly nutritious legumes, and four hundred acres were harvested.

The combination of the moldboard plow's conquest of the European plains, and the introduction of the three-field crop rotation spurred increases in wealth, power, and culture.

Without those advances, Western Europe's economy might not have been ready for Gutenberg's revolutionary InfoTech invention in the fifteenth century.

Charlemagne's war against ignorance

Roman Catholic Church monasteries in the darkest of the "Dark Ages" prevented the complete collapse of intellectual life.

The church's internationally renowned monastery schools laid the groundwork for a coming golden age of literature and learning in an England that was gradually becoming a united kingdom.

It was to England's scholars that Charlemagne—the illiterate king of the Franks—turned for help in 781. He was fortunate to find one of the few Catholic scholars who emphasized science and dialectical logic.

In York, the monk Alcuin's liberal arts and sciences (LAS) school had become widely recognized for its excellence.

Together, the *trivium* and the *quadrivium* comprised its seven liberal arts.

Preparatory work, the *trivium's* language arts included the studies of *grammar, rhetoric,* and *logic.*

Then the *quadrivium's* Real Art—"the four ways"— moved on to the studies of:

- *arithmetic*—math applied to basic numbers
- *geometry*—math applied to space
- *music*—math applied to the time and sound of harmonics and tuning
- *astronomy*—math applied to heavenly time and space.

(Professor Hart notes that the quadrivium is fundamentally the trivium with logic/math. It wasn't until late in life that I became aware of the vital link between math and harmonics. I've since noticed how common it is for scientists to enjoy music as a hobby, as did Albert Einstein.)

Soon after Alcuin's scholarly fame reached the continent, Charlemagne convinced the monk to join his palace to help launch the Carolingian Renaissance.

Alcuin brought to France his works on grammar, chronology—the science that deals with measuring time by regular divisions and assigns to events their proper dates—and biblical studies. Along with other works from English monasteries, they contributed greatly to a rebirth of scholarship on the continent.

Despite being illiterate—or maybe because of it—Charlemagne was a champion of the liberal arts and sciences, even though he may have been too old to advance personally very far in such studies.

Became the Holy Roman Emperor

Charlemagne, who had expanded the Frankish kingdoms into a Frankish Empire that incorporated much of Western and Central Europe, ruled the Holy Roman Empire from 800 until his death in 814.

He and his successor, Louis the Pious, oversaw reforms in the church, the courts, and government, as well as enrichments in the fields of literature, writing, the arts, architecture, liturgical, and scriptural studies. The bartering system was also transformed.

Many of those reforms impacted trade, court, writing, and governmental records systems. Possibly even more significant was the rapid increase in the number of liberal arts colleges throughout the world.

Many historians title this period of cultural and intellectual revival the Carolingian Renaissance. Some, however, contend that the majority of changes it brought about were confined almost entirely to the clergy and spawned no wide ranging social movements, such as the one developed in the later Italian Renaissance.

Invasions by Vikings, Magyars, and Saracens from east, north, west, and south led to the breakup of the Carolingian Empire in the ninth century, and its renaissance faded away.

No doubt major factors in its disappearance were the instability brought about by the invaders and their destruction of so many of the manuscripts Carolingian scholars had produced.

Also, without such major information technologies as paper and print, the Carolingian Renaissance lacked the means to share widely information about its advances.

Carolingian miniscule a unifying factor

Charlemagne had recruited Alcuin not just to spearhead the Carolingian Renaissance in the eighth century but also to achieve culturally unifying standardization across the Carolingian Empire.

Until then—even though using the same language—people wrote as well as spoke in different dialects. That made it difficult for them to communicate with each other. Charlemagne's empire was the first to deal with this issue.

As abbot of the St. Martin at Tours Abbey, the monk from York oversaw the creation of a most helpful information technology—the Carolingian miniscule script.

A revolutionary writing style, it made it much easier for the small but vital literate populations in different regions to communicate with each other in Latin. It became the standard in Europe.

Today, we take for granted its spaces between words, punctuation marks, CAPITAL letters, and lowercase letters with ascenders and descenders.

To experience how difficult reading print might be without such improvements, here's a sentence in a pre-Carolingian format, though in Latin and without the helpful ascenders (on b, d, etc.) and descenders (on g, p, etc.):

thissentencewouldhavehadnocapitallettersandnospacesbetweenwords andnoteventheseascendersordescendersbeforecarolingianminuscule

Here's the same sentence converted to Alcuin's Carolingian format—with spaces, capital letters, ascenders and descenders:

This sentence would have had no capital letters and no spaces between words—and not even ascenders or descenders—before Carolingian minuscule.

Had not Charlemagne recruited that creative York monk into the court of his Holy Roman Empire, reading and writing skills might not have accelerated the advance of Western Civilization.

Most of us learned to write with capitals, spaces, ascenders, and descenders. We were never told that the alphabetic language had been used for thousands of years without the benefit of those helpful innovations.

CHAPTER 9

Illiterate tribes of nomad herder-hunters
took less than a century to forge
the largest contiguous empire
in the history of the world.
—Jack Weatherford

Largest Land Empire Ever

Positive achievements of the Mongol Empire have long been celebrated in Central Asia, but historians in the West paid them little attention until late in the twentieth century.

In less than one century, illiterate tribes of nomad herder-hunters assembled and unified the largest contiguous empire in the history of the world—one that's never been matched.

The Mongols then swung open for just one century the gates between the Orient and the West that had blocked direct human traffic and the sharing of knowledge for millennia.

These fierce warriors once threatened to overrun Europe, but late in the thirteenth century, their leaders unfettered East-West traffic and trade. The resulting exchanges of goods and ideas, including Information Technologies, would nourish Europe's then-embryonic Renaissance.

To set the stage for this almost incredible tale with its similarly implausible climax, our InfoTech trail resurfaces in northeast Asia near the end of the twelfth century.

Jack Weatherford, in his page-turner biography *Genghis Khan and the Making of the Modern World*, details how the genius and character of the Mongol leader enabled him to create what may be history's most amazing empire.

Mongolian climates challenge man and beast

The Pacific Ocean's moisture-bearing winds water the lush coastal plains of Asia's agrarian civilizations. North of the 45-degree parallel, winds blow mostly from the Arctic northwest across the interior Asian plateau and release what little moisture they carry onto the northern Khenti Mountain Range. That leaves dry the huge terrain to the south known as the Gobi Desert.

Between the harsh desert and the moderately watered mountains to the north, vast stretches of steppe turn green after summer rains. Lured by their lushness, nomads would move along rolling steppes in search of grass to nourish their herds.

In the nomadic rhythm of the steppes, the Mongols spent spring tending newborn animals; summer, searching for green pastures; fall, drying meat and dairy products; and the long and cold winter, hunting.

At the end of the first millennium AD, those steppes were home to dozens of tribes and clans, most of them linked genetically. On the west, the Mongols' closest neighbors were the Turkic tribes. To the east lay the Tatars (or Tartars) and Khitans.

All spoke Altaic languages distantly similar to Korean and Japanese but different from Chinese and other Asian tonal languages. (Even today, Turks in Anatolia easily master Korean and Japanese.)

Mongol tribes considered lowly scavengers

Other steppe tribes considered the Mongols scavengers because their steppes lacked enough grassland to feed large herds. The Mongols hunted small animals and—given the chance—stole livestock and women from neighbor tribes on the grassier steppes.

The Mongol male was perfectly attuned to a natural cycle of raiding other tribes and defending his own tribal possessions from raids by his neighbors.

The entire tribe's future depended heavily upon its men of fighting age. Since men stood the best chance of being killed in any raid, whenever their tribe was surprised by an attack, they'd mount the best horses and flee, leaving behind most of the tribe's animals and material goods. The attackers rarely pursued.

The raiders would take young women as wives and young boys as slaves. Older women and the youngest children were usually exempt from harm.

If the escaping men managed to summon allies quickly enough, they'd double back to pursue attackers hoping to recover their goods. If not, the defeated tribesmen rounded up animals that had eluded the captors and reorganized their lives, nourishing plans for a counterattack at a more propitious time.

For the Mongols, fighting was more of a cyclical system of raiding than true warfare.

Prestige for the victor was based on goods brought back and shared with family and friends. The victors didn't collect heads or scalps. Nor did they cut notches hailing the number of killed. Only the goods mattered, not honor in battle.

This culture kept the level of violence low but perpetuated tribal conflict.

Virtually all male Mongols became warriors

Boys began riding before they could walk. The raiding and the need to defend their possessions required that they quickly learn to shoot a rapid stream of arrows with a composite bow while they rode ponies.

Temüjin, who would become the legendary Genghis Khan, was born in 1162 and grew up in a violent tribal world of murder, kidnapping, and enslavement.

Still in his twenties, Temüjin acted to end the Mongols' historic steppe cycle of tribal attacks and counterattacks. After his first victory, he demanded—and received—the losers' promise to join him in future wars. In return, he withdrew from their territory.

Nevrtheless, when they betrayed that promise, Temüjin assembled a jury of his followers to conduct a public trial of the defeated tribe's aristocratic leaders. After the guilty verdict was rendered, Temüjin had them executed.

He then occupied their territory and redistributed the tribe's remaining members among the households of his own clan. Rather than make them slaves, he made them members of his tribe in good standing.

Temüjin's two messages to the steppes were clear as mountain water:

- "Follow me faithfully and receive rewards and good treatment.
- Choose to attack me, and you can expect no mercy!"

This became his policy for his lifetime.

By 1204, he had defeated every Mongol tribe and removed the threat of every tribe's aristocratic lineage by killing off their men and marrying their women to his sons and other followers.

Taking the name Genghis Khan, he quickly moved to establish all the institutions needed by this new state of *Yeke Mongol Ulus* (Great Mongol Nation).

Illiterate Khan respected writing's power

Although himself illiterate, Genghis Khan was quick to grasp the importance of the written word. To ensure that his laws would be preserved accurately and without alteration for generations, he ordered his top aides to learn to read and write.

(He foreshadowed Gutenberg when he ordered the adaptation of a thirty-eight-character alphabetic script from the Uigur Turks. That enabled Mongols to devise a print system using movable type—wooden rather than metal.)

To establish peace and order, he had Draconian laws drawn up to end the continual robbery and blood feuds on the steppes. Traditional local laws remained in effect so long as they did not conflict with the Great Law.

His new laws

- Set the death penalty for robbery and adultery,
- Put an end to slavery (from which he himself had suffered),
- Banned the selling of women into marriage, and
- Declared all children legitimate, and
- Made animal rustling a capital offense.

Genghis Khan recognized the disruptive potential of competing religions and—more than five hundred years before the United States adopted its Bill of Rights—decreed complete and total religious freedom for everyone.

One of his first moves was to organize the Mongol military into units of ten, one hundred, one thousand, and ten thousand. He broke up the old tribal units and spread their warriors among the decimal units, selecting leaders on merit alone. He did this to assure that loyalties would be to the Mongol Army and his leadership rather than to the old tribal ties.

The army's tactics avoided risky frontal assaults and used instead diversionary tactics that enabled its main forces to outflank the enemy. Leaders—too valuable to be exposed recklessly—directed the battles with signal flags and horns from atop hills away from the action.

Captives with no skills might be assigned to help in the attack on the next city by carrying loads, digging fortifications, serving as human shields, or being pushed into moats as fill. Those unqualified for any of the above were either slaughtered or left behind.

Early on, Genghis Khan saw that the common people cared little about the idle rich, so his armies killed all the enemy aristocrats as quickly as possible in order to forestall having to wage future wars against them.

Mongols launch three-decade expansion

Genghis Khan's immediate predecessor had offered his allegiance to the Jurched Dynasty that ruled northern China, Manchuria, and much of modern-day Inner Mongolia.

After Genghis Khan had spent about four years consolidating his new nation, the Jurched's newly enthroned Golden Khan demanded that the Mongols submit as a subject nation. That gave Genghis Khan the excuse he needed to assemble a council of his leaders to approve his call to war.

His decision to cross the Gobi and invade the Jurched territory unleashed the Mongol warriors to begin a series of historic conquests that drastically changed the world.

In the next thirty years, Mongol armies would overrun everything from the Indus River to the Danube and from the Pacific Ocean to the Mediterranean.

The Mongols promised justice to those who surrendered but swore destruction to those who resisted. Those who subjugated themselves and offered friendship in such ways as donating food were treated as members of the Mongol family with guaranteed protection and certain familial rights. Those who refused to surrender subjected themselves, their wives, children, and dependents to possible horrifying treatment.

First, the Mongols killed the soldiers—so as not to leave an army of enemies blocking the route to their Mongolia homeland. Then the captured were divided by their occupation:

- Professionals—those who could read or write in any language— doctors, astronomers, judges, soothsayers, engineers, teachers, imams, rabbis, or priests.
- Merchants, cameleers, craftsmen, and those who spoke multiple languages.

Barbaric as Mongol warrior customs were, their methods differed significantly from those the Islamic Turks used to terrorize their enemies. Although the Mongols did kill at an unprecedented rate and used death to create terror, they did not torture, mutilate, or maim their captives.

The Legacy of Genghis Khan

To instill fear in his enemies, Genghis Khan created a propaganda machine that consistently inflated the number of people his warriors killed in battle; however, he had no interest in hearing elaborate praise of his own prowess, and no portraits of him exist.

Nevertheless, eight centuries after his empire terrorized two continents, the Great Khan is still revered by Mongolians. Named for him are many a newborn baby, streets, and schools as well as a brand of vodka. In the nation's capital, twenty-first-century projects include the Genghis Khan Airport and a five-million-dollar statue of him and his sons.

When Genghis Khan died in 1227:

- His armies were undefeated,

- His empire stretched from the Pacific Ocean to the Caspian Sea, and
- His realm was twice the size of the Roman Empire at its peak.

The Mongol Empire almost doubled in size under the rule of his descendants, and it became the largest contiguous empire in the history of the world.

Mongols grew history's largest contiguous empire[10]

In less than one century, illiterate tribes of nomad herder-hunters assembled and unified the largest contiguous empire in the history of the world—one that's never been matched.

Twice the size of the Roman Empire when Genghis Khan died, the Mongol Empire almost doubled in size under the rule of his descendants to become the largest contiguous empire in the history of the world.

At its greatest extent, it spanned six thousand miles, covered an area equal to 22 percent of the Earth's total land area, and held sway over a population of a hundred million.

---

10   Search Google images for "MongolEmpire.jpg" (stet) and Wikipedia for "Genghis Kahn"

CHAPTER 10

Then for a single century … that curtain
was lifted, and there was direct human
contact between Europe and China.
—Daniel J. Boorstin (1914–2004)

Mongols Open the Way

Three decades after the death of Genghis Khan, strife among his descendants threatened the stability of the Mongol Empire he had created. The victor in the family civil war was a grandson able and powerful enough to take that empire to even greater heights.

Only twelve in 1927 when his grandfather died, by 1259 Kublai Khan had matured into a ruler ready to unite and lead the empire forward. By granting family members considerable independence in the governance of other territories, he was able to remain Chief Khan of the Mongols while he concentrated on expanding into China and became its emperor.

Kublai Khan's greatest legacy from Genghis Khan was this tradition his grandfather had established in the Mongol military: He never asked his men to die for him and never willingly sacrificed a single one.

The Mongols' only goal was victory. Brave warriors won no honor if the battle was lost. Nor did clever deception or cruel trickery leave any stains on a warrior's bravery.

The empire's founder adapted the tribal battle tactics of his mounted nomad hunters to wage war against civilized nations:

- Each warrior carried only what he needed.
- A large reserve of horses and goatherds always accompanied the all-cavalry army.
- No cumbersome supply train slowed its progress.

Riding bareback on range-bred, pony-size mounts, the Mongols overwhelmed their foes in well-coordinated attacks.

Their bows shot rapid-fired streams of arrows, and some could kill at two hundred yards. The construction of each of the composite bows required an average of four months because the bows needed three or four different materials for construction. These included special types of wood, pieces of horn, and sinew crafted together.

Even though it took less energy to pull and release their bowstrings, these shorter bows transferred more energy to the arrows than did ordinary bows.

By the time Kublai Khan was ready to begin his drive to control all of China, the Mongol Army had mastered ways to conquer fortified towns and cities. Captured engineers directed the building and testing of siege machines which then would be disassembled and carried by horses to battle sites where they could be swiftly reassembled.

Silk Road gift kept on giving

One of Genghis Khan's largest gifts to his people was access to the Silk Road.

Linked to China, India, Persia, and Mediterranean nations, its twisting channels of commerce had lain so far south that little of the wealth they carried ever reached the Mongol Nation.

After he rerouted them northward across the Mongol steppes, he collected them into a single stream of carts carrying coveted cargo flowing out of China.

In addition to colorful silk fabrics, the wide variety of goods included paper fans, porcelain bowls, robes embroidered with silver and golden thread, iron kettles, brass pots, and carved saddles.

The Mongols established a system of fast riders known as arrow messengers across Mongolia five centuries before America's "pony express."

Besides embracing the Mongol military tradition and stressing the importance of a safe Silk Road, Kublai Khan also replicated his grandfather's practice of religious tolerance.

Combined genius, courage and tolerance

In *The Discoverers*, his epic history of *Man's Search to Know the World and Himself*, the late librarian of Congress Daniel J. Boorstin wrote:

"When Kublai Khan came to the Mongol throne in 1260, his empire reached from the Yellow River in China to the shores of the Danube in eastern Europe and from Siberia to Vietnam and the Persian Gulf.

"The Mongol Khans, from Genghis Khan through his sons and grandsons ... were as able a dynasty as ever ruled a great empire. They showed a combination of military genius, personal courage, and cultural tolerance unequaled by any European line of hereditary rulers.

"They deserve a higher place and a different place than they have been given by the Western historian."

In his highly praised *The Middle East: A Brief History of the Last 2,000 Years*, Bernard Lewis seems to concur. He writes that the Mongol khans in Iran "encouraged the reconstruction of town life, industry and trade, fostered what they consider useful sciences, and ... even Islamic literature and learning."

In his chapter on "How the Mongols Opened the Way," Boorstin notes that prior to the thirteenth-century merchants from Venice, Genoa, Pisa, or Paris prospered selling luxuries, such as sleek Chinese silk, diamonds from Golconda, and costly Persian carpets.

Islamic officials, however, blocked their way to China or India. Similarly, Frankish or Italian merchants were stopped as soon as they tried to travel eastward from the Mediterranean ports, where trading of goods from the Orient terminated.

Free-Trade Mongols open East-West gate

The Khans believed in free trade among nations.

When the gate that blocked East from West came under their control during the second half of the thirteenth century, the Mongols opened the Silk Road to two-way traffic.

To make merchants welcome, they eliminated trade barriers, maintained post stations, lowered tolls and taxes, protected caravans against bandits, and instituted the use of paper money.

Safe transit of goods and ideas between East and West led to an unprecedented rise in trade and cultural communication.

In that special century between 1250 and 1350 AD, shared knowledge and human contacts flowed between China and Europe. Travelers to and from the Orient included not just merchants but also artists, diplomats, doctors, scholars, scientists, and priests from all religions, including Catholics, Nestorians, Armenians, Buddhists, and Muslims.

Kublai Khan's reign spawned numerous developments in Chinese culture. Besides allowing religious freedom, he created aid agencies, reorganized and improved roads, and expanded waterways.

Chinese civilization during the rule of Kublai Khan surpassed anything in the rest of the world by such a margin that readers in the West were simply dazzled by Marco Polo's vivid account of extensive travels on behalf of the Khan during twenty-four years in Asia.[11]

Kublai welcomed European merchants, travelers, and missionaries from different orders to his court. He sent and received envoys to and from centers as distant as Rome and London.

But the Silk Road traffic remained two-way for one century only.

In the second half of the fourteenth century, both Mongol rule in China and Mongol control of the East-West gateway ended.

Although the dynasty founded by Genghis Khan would survive in Mongolia into the seventeenth century, direct European contact with China did not, and indirect contact between Europe and China declined to pre-Mongol levels.

Seeking another Silk Route to China

Tremendous profits were to be obtained by anyone who could innovate a direct trade connection with Asia. Closing the overland gate spurred the Europeans to find another path to the prosperous Chinese empire.

---

11 Some suggest that Polo never went to China with his father and his uncle but plagiarized his reports from other travelers' stories.

The seaways offered real advantages over land routes. In that era, "travel" by land was so rigorous that it lived up to "travail," its root word that defined "arduous or painful effort."

When Christopher Columbus sailed west in 1492, he reportedly wished to create yet another Silk Route to China. Before he recognized the potential of a "New World," he was upset that he had reached a continent "in between" Europe and the Orient.

Boorstin first suggests that—without the Mongol rulers' "peculiar talents"—there might never have been a path for Marco Polo Then he asks, "Without Marco Polo and the others who stirred the European imagination with impatience to reach Cathay, would there have been a Christopher Columbus?"

Polo's book was first printed fifteen years before Columbus's first voyage to America. The great navigator's son, Ferdinand, founded the Columbian Library at Seville, where his father's copy may still be seen. He said his father kept the book with him constantly.

Others, however, favor the idea that Columbus's westward Atlantic crossing more likely stemmed from his encounters with sailors who had touched the American continent.

In his revealing *COD: A Biography of the Fish that Changed the World*, Mark Kurlansky contends that—for centuries before Columbus—Basque fisherman kept secret their profitable catches of cod on regular trips to American waters.

Mongols fostered exchange of ideas and inventions

The Mongols made no technological breakthroughs, founded no new religions, wrote few books or dramas, and gave the world no new crops or methods of agriculture.

Yet the Mongols' disseminated knowledge from one civilization to the next on a grand scale. Their armies conquered culture after culture and, along the way, shared all the skills they gathered.

Ideas and inventions flow westward

In earlier chapters, we've encountered Information Technology, such as paper and block printing, which later gave birth to equally revolutionary InfoTech.

Arrival in the West of the Chinese inventions of gunpowder and the compass revolutionized warfare and made possible the voyages east to India and the Pacific as well as west to the Americas.

Printed playing cards were among the examples of Chinese block printing on textiles and paper that reached northern Europe. Some reports indicate that they inspired Johann Gutenberg and his competitors in the early fifteenth century to create movable metal type.

West marvels at Oriental riches

Perhaps of at least equal importance, the riches of the Orient stimulated Western desires for luxuries and opened the door to capitalism.

Summarizing the role of the Mongols, H.G. Wells may have said it best:

"This story of Mongolian conquests is surely one of the most remarkable in all history. The conquests of Alexander the Great cannot compare with them in extent.

"For that time in the 1200s and 1300s all Asia and Western Europe enjoyed an open intercourse; all the roads were temporarily open, and representatives of every nation (e.g., Marco Polo) appeared at the Court of Karakorum. That brief time lowered the barriers between Europe and Asia that the religious feud between Islam and Christianity had erected.

"The effect in diffusing and broadening men's ideas and stimulating their imaginations was enormous."

'Savage hordes' opened East-West trade

Terrified by reports of the devastating Mongol invasions that leveled whole cities and massacred millions, most in the West viewed the Mongol armies as "savage hordes lusting after gold, women and blood." Mongol warriors may have also brought the Black Death that devastated Europe.

By opening a path through barriers that had isolated Europe from the Orient for centuries, however, that Mongol warrior nation:

- Set flowing freely for one spirited century a stream of ideas and inventions from the Pacific to the Atlantic.
- Produced an umbilical cord that nourished the developing embryo of Europe's glorious Renaissance with the power of shared knowledge.
- Accelerated the West's later rise to world dominance, and
- Stimulated a historic quest in the West for more knowledge and innovation that continues to this very day.

Mongols opened Silk Road's west gates [12]

For just a single significant century the Mongols swung open the gates that for so long had blocked direct human traffic—and the sharing of knowledge—between the Orient and the West.

By turning the historic Silk Road into an intellectual and commercial artery, they produced an umbilical cord that nourished the developing embryo of Europe's glorious Renaissance with the power of shared knowledge.

That flow of new ideas and inventions from the Orient during midthirteenth and fourteenth centuries stimulated a historic quest in the West for more knowledge and innovation that continues to this very day.

Under Kublai Khan, Chinese civilization surpassed anything in the rest of the world by such a margin that readers in the West were simply dazzled by Marco Polo's vivid account of extensive travels on behalf of the Khan during twenty-four years in Asia.

Kublai welcomed European merchants, travelers, and missionaries from different orders to his court, and he sent and received envoys to and from centers as distant as Rome and London.

---

12 Search Google images for "Silk Road" and Wikipedia for "Kublai Khan"

CHAPTER 11

If only he (Archimedes) had made that discovery!
To what heights science would have risen by now?
—Johann Carl Friedrich Gaus (1777–1855),
"the prince of mathematicians"

The Missing Keys to the Science Chest

If the alphabet is "man's greatest invention," then its runner-up must be the numeral system we call Arabic with the once-missing invisible number.

Just as the alphabet's advantages tower over pictorial writing's shortcomings, so too do Arabic numerals prove infinitely easier to manipulate than Roman numerals. Do you remember learning the following equivalents in grade school?

1=I, 5=V, 10=X, 50=L, 100=C, 500=D, and 1000=M

In some cases, we could subtract by placing a smaller value before a larger one: IX = 10 - 1 = 9. But Roman math rules were complex.

Fractions did not exist in Roman numerals, so words spelled some of them but not all of them. They also had no zero, but some mathematicians in the Middle Ages used the word "nulla" (Latin for none) in their calculations.

Imagine trying to use them to multiply and divide. The Greeks managed to calculate pi's 3.141592, but it must have been enormously difficult.

Zero's power hidden for millennia

Nothing in decades of episodic research into past Information Technologies startled me more than reading Charles Seife's captivating and enlightening *Zero: The Biography of a Dangerous Idea*.

In that book, Seife reasons that since our children learn to count before they learn the ABCs, our ancestors probably learned to count before they learned to write.

Many thousands of years ago—when Homo sapiens cut notches in wolf bones to count—logic must have told them the first notch represented the first number. Hence, none of the earliest counting systems started on empty.

It probably never occurred to them that the smooth wolf bone was empty of notches before they cut the first notch. Even today, some primitive tribes still start counting: "One and one" and then "one and many" but never "nothing and one."

Fear of void stalled science

Seife contends that for almost two thousand years, the advance of Western science stalled because ancient Greek mathematicians thought zero was a dangerous idea.

Those Greeks believed that only emptiness and darkness prevailed before the universe. That gave birth to a primal fear of void and chaos that enveloped nothingness and the idea of zero.

Zero also seemed to the Greeks to violate the mathematics' rules.

Add or subtract zero, and nothing changes. Multiply or divide any number by zero, and the answer is zero.

Similarly, famed Greek mathematicians, who specialized in the geometry of areas and volumes, thought it a silly exercise to try to subtract three acres from two acres.

Babylonians created zero as a placeholder when they inscribed an abacus on a clay tablet, but the very idea of any void spooked the early Greeks.

All modern mathematics— math beyond geometry— fixes the zero as the starting linchpin in plus and minus sequences.

History of the missing number hazy

Mathematicians find the zero, which denotes "nothing," to be almost incalculably valuable, but its history, along with that of the decimal-place system we use today, is hazy.

It is clear, however, that Babylonians used an abacus with zero represented by any row with no pebble at the active end of the rod.

Because the Hindu spiritual world came out of nothingness, it seems natural that Hindus borrowed from the Babylonians' numbering process. For certain, our word "zero" stems from its Hindu roots.

As noted earlier, Islam created an empire that stretched from China to France while the West was declining after Rome's fall. After the Muslims conquered India, they were quick to absorb the wisdom of that culture, which did not fear the void.

The Hindus had figured out how to use their new numeral system for fancy tricks. They could add, subtract, multiply, and divide quickly without an abacus. Expressing every possible number using a set of ten symbols—each of which had a place value and an absolute value—so simplified calculations that mathematicians soon revolutionized the nature of science.

Arabs appropriated this simple system from Hindu mathematicians and then carried it to the West.

By the time this ingenious math system finally reached Europe, it had long been in common use from Libya to Morocco. That's probably why we call them "Arabic numerals." Arabs themselves, however, connect them to their origin and call the system "Hindu numerals."

At first, the Arabic numbering system encountered considerable skepticism in Europe. It mattered not to Christians that their Bible told of creation from the void. Many still looked upon zero as "dangerous Saracen magic!"

In 1202, a book written by Leonardo of Pisa—*Liber Abaci*—explained how much easier Arabic numbers could handle complex calculations, as opposed to Roman numerals such as IX or XVII.

Double-entry bookkeeping spurs world trade

Italians took Arabic numerals another step forward when they used them to invent double-entry bookkeeping. One simply enters credits and debts on the same page in parallel columns and then totals both columns.

The books balance if the difference is zero. Imbalances indicate profits or losses. Simplifying accounting by introducing double-entry bookkeeping set Italy's world trade soaring.

Bankers were major beneficiaries, because this new mathematical tool let them dispense with their counting boards.

The new commercial vocabulary inspired thinking in ways previously unimaginable. Scientists, for instance, would frame comprehensive laws in physics stating that matter, momentum, and energy neither created nor destroyed but exchanged.

In the 1400s Arabic numerals spread through Europe at about the same time paper mills began producing inexpensive paper, the best material for doing calculations with this modern numbering system.

The foundations were in place. Now the structure of modern science could rise.

"How could he have missed it?"

Johann Carl Friedrich Gauss (1777–1855) was dubbed the prince of mathematicians. One of the greatest of all time, he was an admirer of Archimedes, the Greek who mastered the math of areas and volumes and founded the science of hydraulics in Aristotle's time.

In the mid-1800s, however, Gauss decried Archimedes's failure two millennia earlier to adopt the convenient notation for the powers of ten built into the zero. Gauss asked sorrowfully:

"How could he have missed it? If only he had made that discovery! To what heights science would have risen by now?"

Calendars and Centuries Still Untidy

When Homo sapiens first marked bones and sticks with slashes, they quite logically called the first slash "one"—skipping over the smooth (zero) surface in their counts.

Holdovers from that beginning of numbering and the Greek fear of a void continue to impact our present day numbering systems.

Just look at the numbers across the top of your computer keyboards—zero follows nine:

1 2 3 4 5 6 7 8 9 0

But the numerical keyboard at the bottom right gets it right:

7 8 9
4 5 6
1 2 3
0

It makes little or no difference that the first day of our months are all one instead of zero. But when we talk about centuries, it makes an annoying difference.

From 1 AD to 99 AD is our first century because we lack a zero century. So we call 100 AD to 199 AD the second century, 200 to 299 the third, etc.

Consequently, we have to figure a bit to realize 1776 falls in the eighteenth rather than the seventeenth, and 1929—the start of the Great Depression—falls in the twentieth.

At the turn into this century, that complexity generated this spirited but never-settled debate topic:

Did January 1, 2000, mark the end of the twentieth century or the beginning of the twenty-first?

CHAPTER 12

Over centuries, Norse and Anglo-Saxon tongues came together and became Britain's dominant language. Then the Normans added French to that mix.

Invaders from the North

We now step back in time and then jump over in space to the British Isles to view the evolution of an Information Technology—a special language—destined to play a surprisingly influential role in the rise of Western Civilization.

Julius Caesar's Roman Legions found no sign of any written language on the island when they first raided southern Britain in 54 and 55 BC, but most of the island natives spoke the Celtic tongue. Crossing over from central Europe to Britain and Ireland, their Celts ancestors had laid the Indo-European seedbed for the English language's first roots.

The huge Roman province of Britannia stretched as far north as southern Scotland by 300 AD, but Lincoln Barnett writes in *The Treasure of Our Tongue* that soon thereafter: "The golden afternoon of the Roman occupation—when the countryside lay at peace, dotted with opulent villas surrounded by fertile fields and park-like pastures—had begun to darken."

Barbarian natives from the north periodically ruptured such defenses as the seventy-three-mile-long Hadrian's Wall and put pressure on the twenty thousand Roman troops on the island.

Soon, new waves of Teutonic invaders—fierce warriors swinging huge battleaxes—crossed the North Sea in beaked longboats. They burned and plundered towns and villages.

Meanwhile, the entire Roman Empire began to crumble. Travel on its famous roads became unsafe, and barbarians threatened on every border. Its political and financial systems were foundering.

By 410 AD, the empire had abandoned Britannia primarily to free its legions to defend Italy from the Visigoths' attacks.

Britannia's Golden Age

Winston Churchill would write that Britain, during the Roman occupation, "enjoyed in many respects the happiest, most comfortable ... time its inhabitants have ever had ... well-to-do persons in Britain lived better than they would again until the twentieth century."

Wealthy British-Roman citizens built into their country houses a hypocaust central heating system with underground furnaces and tile flues to distribute the heat.

But for fifteen hundred years after the Romans departed, the cold of unheated dwellings prevailed, mitigated only by occasional roasts before gigantic wasteful fires. Baths disappeared until the mid-nineteenth century.

Three centuries after the Roman Legions had left for good, many in the Celtic population still called themselves Romani and considered the legionnaires' language to be their language. Known as "vulgar" Latin, it was the speech of the middle class in most Roman provinces.

Yet few Latin-derivative words in today's English trace their ancestry to the Roman occupation. The majority, by far, came down secondhand through other languages that would arrive later from the continent.

Angles, Saxons and Jutes come in waves

The cradle of the English we speak rocked in the homelands of invading Germanic tribes.

About the time the Romans were pulling up stakes from their Britannia, the Angles, the Saxons, and the Jutes began launching raids across the North Sea from northern Germany and the Jutland (Danish) peninsula.

Each wave brought more seeds of Teutonic speech.

Later, these invaders built permanent settlements, gained control of most of the island, and renamed it England. ("Englaland" had been the Angles homeland in the south of the Danish peninsula. Similarly, their "Englisc" language became English.)

Not imposed by force but rather absorbed over time by the conquered Britons, the invaders' tongue became the dominant language of Britain. Linguist Sir Brooke Boothly writes that English "completely supplanted Latin (save in the Church) and drove the Celtic tongue forever to the north and west."

The evolution of English down to the present time has been a continuous process—a march in the direction of ever increasing simplicity and flexibility, unbroken for 1,500 years."

By the end of the eighth century, England was approaching unity and entering a golden age of literature and learning, one led primarily by the Roman Catholic Church's internationally renowned monastery schools on the British islands.

Two-pronged invasion from the North

From the eighth through the eleventh centuries, fierce warriors began a series of invasions into both England and France down along two corridors from the north—one down the English Channel and the other via land along the Europe's west coast.

These invading Norsemen plundered British monasteries and prompted monks to pray:

From the fury of the Norsemen deliver us, O Lord!"

Vikings forayed across the Atlantic to North America centuries before Columbus stole the historic limelight, but their impact upon the English language may have been more significant than their westward forays.

Alfred the Great, king of Wessex (871–99), the first Saxon king to declare himself "King of the English," stalled the invaders advance, but only for a few decades. A century later Canute became the first Norse ruler to declare himself England's king, but he also ruled as king of the Danes and Norwegians.

English keeps 'borrowing" more tongues

Over centuries, Norse and Anglo-Saxon tongues mingled to become Britain's dominant language. The merger both simplified the grammar of Anglo-Saxon English and added greatly to its lexicon.

After the Norman invasion in 1066, William the Conqueror's reign grafted other Scandinavian tongues onto an English language already mingled with those of their Viking cousins on the island.

The French language of King William's Norman courtiers may have had even greater impact on the evolution of English. King Richard, the great-grandson of William, was the epitome of a medieval English king, but the Lionhearted spoke only French and spent more time in southwestern France or on crusade than in England.

English continued to develop as a "borrowing" language of great flexibility and ever-increasing vocabulary. It remained in flux even after Gutenberg's historic InfoTech invention set the stage for it to evolve into *The Treasure of Our Tongue*. English would encourage the sharing of knowledge in a manner conducive to the success of democracy.

CHAPTER 13

This we rhymed in school:
Columbus sailed the ocean blue
in fourteen-hundred-and-ninety-two!

This rhyme's just as cool:
Literacy began to soar
in fourteen-hundred-and-fifty-four!

He Unchained Books

The papyrus-and-parchment-manuscript culture prevailed for thousands of years, but by the fifteenth century the stage was set for a historic shift to paper and printing.

In Europe, centuries of progress fueled by the moldboard plow and the three-field planting system had brought considerable economic stability, and the Black Death pandemic had peaked near the middle of the fourteenth century just before the first Italian paper mills opened.

In the aftermath of the plague's killing somewhere of between 30 and 60 percent of Europe's population, rags from the victims' closets created such a surplus of raw material that the capacity of Europe's first paper mills outside of Islamic Spain outgrew the market for scribal writing material.

That resulted in much lower prices for paper, but scripted books remained so labor intensive—and thus so costly—that only royalty, the church, and the very wealthy could afford them.

Books were still so precious that libraries linked them to desks with metal chains to prevent theft. One had to stand at the desk to read such a book.

Since as early as 1424 in the Netherlands—and the early 1440s in Italy and France—craftsmen had been trying to wed the twenty-six-letter phonetic alphabet to a process similar to the movable metal type process that the hundreds of characters in Korean script doomed. The alphabet that made the pen mightier than the sword was about to be harnessed to a new technology that would enable the West to catch up with—and then surpass—the China that had dazzled Marco Polo.

Goldsmith inventor was no businessman

Johann Gensfleisch Zur Laden Zum Gutenberg[13] was born about 1400 in the archbishopric of Mainz, Germany, where his patrician parents reportedly had high-level family connections in the archbishop's court.

It's ironic, but this goldsmith sire of capitalism lacked even a modicum of good financial sense.

His shortcoming first came to light in Mainz. There Gutenberg's tinkering had produced a polished mirror he boasted could capture "holy light" from religious relics. Displays of such relics from Holy Roman Emperor Charlemagne were to be exhibited in the nearby city of Aachen at a fair expected to attract hordes of pilgrims.

Looking to reap a huge profit selling his mirrors to the pilgrims, Gutenberg borrowed heavily to manufacture a large quantity of mirrors. But the fair was canceled, ending any hope for profits from sales of his mirrors.

Rumors hinted that to settle the debt from that luckless venture, Gutenberg promised to share a "secret," presumably his typography invention. Similar secrecy surrounded most early printing ventures. That's probably why historians have found so few records of any other European experiments with movable metal type

End of the script era

Gutenberg's experience tinkering with metals may have given him an edge, but the goldsmith faced stiff competition from a number of rivals. Nevertheless, most scholars agree that in 1454 Johann Gutenberg won that race.

---

13 Born "Johann Gensfleisch" (John Gooseflesh), he preferred to be known as "Johann Gutenberg" (John Beautiful Mountain.

"Printing press" prevails as the popular label for Gutenberg's invention, even though screw-presses set between two upright beams had been used to make wine, cheese, linen, and paper in Europe since the first century AD. Many problems must have been more challenging for him than how to adapt that ancient wine process to press inked letters onto paper.

After all, to create his historic typography system he had to do the following:

- Determine what proportions of lead, antimony, and tin would produce type metal that poured and solidified properly.
- Choose just the right material for the type molds.
- Find an alloy and mold combination to produce type able to withstand printing press pressure and be reused hundreds of times.
- Establish a formula to produce quick-drying ink with a viscosity that did not smear under that same pressure.
- Create fonts of type molds.
- Invent the "printer's stick" and other type-handling tools.

Apparently, Gutenberg solved enough of these problems to convince wealthy moneylender Johann Fust to grant him a large loan and join him in a partnership to produce a Bible.

Gutenberg's apprentice Peter Schoeffer, a calligrapher who would become Fust's son-in-law, joined the partnership. Schoeffer helped oversee the Bible project as well as the more profitable printing of texts, such as Latin grammars and papal indulgences (the forgiveness of sins) for the church.

Historic Bible had two forty-two-line columns

As many as six of the shop's twenty-five or so compositors worked setting two forty-two-line columns on each page of that historic Latin Bible.

Soon after the Bible was finished in 1454, Fust did the following:

- Demanded that Gutenberg repay some of his loans.
- Accused Gutenberg of embezzlement.

- Forced Gutenberg into bankruptcy.
- Took over the print shop, its fonts of type, its inks, and its presses.

In August 1457, the Fust-Schoeffer shop published the Mainz Psalter, the first dated text labeled with its printer's name. Fust touted the revolutionary technology used to produce the book without mentioning his former partner Gutenberg's role in its development.

The Fust-Schoeffer firm became famous, but Fust died of the plague in 1466.

Gutenberg dies broke and in exile

Out on his own, Gutenberg struggled with episodic printing projects. In his final years, his parents' connections and the fame of his 42-line Bible may have brought him a large enough stipend from the ruling court to let him eke out an existence until his death in 1468.

Gutenberg's perfidious partner had driven him into financial ruin from which he never recovered. He died broke, unheralded, and exiled from the land of his birth.

In the second half of the fifteenth century, printers fanned out from Mainz across what came to be known as the Western world and soon put an end to the chaining of books.

Called "walking encyclopedias," scholars who had wandered from place to place in search of manuscripts they might copy in scattered libraries could now afford to have copies of books sent to them.

Before Gutenberg printed his 42-line Bible, the cost of such a book was about the same as the cost of a family farm.

First fifty years outproduced all script history

It's of little import that so little is known about Gutenberg's personal life, but —famous as his name is—it troubles me to realize that too few recognize just how revolutionary his printing process was.

In his typography's first fifty years, presses printed more books than had been scripted in all history before his invention.

Nor do many today realize what drastic changes it wrought between its beginnings and almost the end of the nineteenth century. In those five centuries, printers poured the foundations upon which rose the frameworks of many revolutionary eras, including:

- The Reformation,
- The Industrial Revolution
- Modern science
- Democracy

The Song of the Printer (See next page) personifies his invention's historic knowledge-sharing power that brought about the most radical changes in intellectual life in all of history and spurred the rise of Western Europe.

Books so precious that
chains linked them to desks [14]

Before Gutenberg, books were so precious that the few libraries open to the public routinely chained their books to desks. To read them, one had to stand in front of the desk, and one was able to move the book only as far as its chain would allow.

The Song of the Printer

Pick and click goes the type in the stick,
As the printer stands at his case;
And one by one as the letters go,
Words are piled up steady and slow.

Steady and slow, but still they grow,
Wonderful words, that without a sound
Traverse the earth to its upmost bound;

Words that shall make the tyrant quake,
Words that can crumble an army's might,
Or treble its strength in a righteous fight.

By Anonymous, from MacKellar's
"The American Printer" 1887

---

14   Search Google images for "Chained Books"

CHAPTER 14

After the fall of Rome, Western culture focused more on guarding than on expanding accumulated knowledge.

Printers as Agents of Change

Just as I was tardy to recognize the historic primacy of spoken language among Information Technologies, the full extent of print's role in the rise of the West escaped my notice for decades.

In her all-encompassing book *The Printing Press as an Agent of Change,* Elizabeth Eisenstein places great emphasis upon printing's transformation of Europe's intellectual culture.

She stresses that pioneer print shops—with their new machines and mechanics trained to operate them—served as:

- Gathering places for scholars, artists, and literati.
- Sanctuaries for foreign translators, émigrés, and refugees.
- Institutions of advanced learning.
- Focal points for every kind of cultural and intellectual interchange.

"Significance (of printing) as a whole"

The flowering of literacy and creativity in Europe after the fifteenth century resulted not just from Gutenberg's revolutionary technology. Print shop culture facilitated its spread immeasurably.

Eisenstein acknowledges that it "makes sense to employ the term Renaissance to a two-phased culture movement ... initiated by Italian literati and artistes in the age of scribes and expanded in the age of print to encompass many regions and fields of study."

She emphasizes, however, the need to differentiate between the Renaissance's launching of a modern consciousness of history and the print industry's setting in motion a major communications revolution.

Eisenstein, moreover, decries an ivory-tower tendency in recent times to chop studies of printing into small curriculum pieces.

For example, she cites allocations of:

- The history of printing to library studies,
- The topic of printing itself to historians of technology, and
- The combination of type design, layout, and lettering to schools of design.

She complains that one "rarely gets a sense of (printing's) significance as a whole" when the topic is "so segmented, subdivided and parceled out."

Print broke chains of ignorance

By breaking the chains of ignorance that held most of mankind in bondage for millennia, Gutenberg's print technology did the following:

- Opened paths to political, scientific, and industrial revolutions.
- Formed the basis of every modern education system.
- Removed from both the church and the state their control over what people might know, because printing made censorship too costly to be effective.
- Nourished literature and was nourished by it—the more there was to read, the more point in learning to read.
- Accelerated the use of Arabic numerals so that they became widely known in Europe before the end of the fifteenth century.

Past preservation priority proved costly

Medieval Western culture focused on guarding rather than on expanding accumulated knowledge. It was more or less heresy to suggest that changing the wording could make it better.

That convention to preserve original writings or drawings was so ingrained that some scribes were forbidden to make *any* corrections. This applied to even the best-educated or experienced scribes.

Such a culture not only preserved errors but also opened the way for copy thus corrupted to be further corrupted when next copied.

Print shops, on the other hand, first republished the bulk of the existing body of knowledge and then used this revolutionary technology to make books of all sorts affordable.[15]

No longer burdened with the boring, tedious, and mistake-prone job of copying, scholars with newfound mental energy were free to expand boundaries for sharing knowledge exponentially.

Huge gain for star-gazers and map-makers

Communications surged among scholars in such different fields of study as mathematics, medicine, botany, biology, zoology, geography, history, and navigation.

Astronomers were quick to welcome freedom from the tedium of copying their own tables that charted the paths of heavenly bodies. Printed tables, moreover, were far less likely to be corrupted.

Almanacs featured uniform tables for computing costs of goods and payments of wages as well as lists converting weights and measures. By the seventeenth century, such books outsold the Bible in England.

We tend to associate printing with text, but engravings of maps and illustrations in how-to books added much to the impact of print. Astronomers fixed star charts and cartographers fixed maps of geographic sites far more precisely with engravings than had been possible before printing.

Book fairs attract print publishers

By the middle of the fifteenth century, outdoor fairs had played a significant economic role in Europe for hundreds of years. Over time, many expanded

---

15 "How to" tomes—as in this modern age were among the early best sellers.

from weekly open-air town markets to multi-day events combined with annual local saints festal celebrations.

As pioneer printers spread out across Europe in the late fifteenth and early sixteenth centuries, they not only opened their own stalls at existing fairs but also staged their own book fairs.

Printers flocked, for instance, to the rival German centers of Frankfurt and Leipzig for major book fairs. Prospective buyers from the growing literate populace, such as scholars, professors, poets, and mathematicians, would gather to interact in a weeklong, intellectual atmosphere.

At Frankfurt, fairgoers had no trouble finding pamphlets of Martin Luther's works. In the seventeenth century, famed mathematician Johannes Kepler promoted his books at the fair.

As time passed, however, publishers found other avenues opened for selling their wares. With only a few exceptions, such as Frankfurt and Leipzig's effort, which survived into the twenty-first century, most book fairs simply disappeared.

Printing as a magical Black Art

In the early days of printing—a time of mass illiteracy—people tended to think anyone skilled in working with metals was an alchemist seeking to magically transform common metals into valuable gold.

That ink-stained shop apprentices came to be known as "printers' devils," which sheds some light on how revolutionary printing must have seemed to Gutenberg and Fust's contemporaries. To them, the shift from script to print seemed magical.

In one report, Fust tried to peddle to the king of France and his courtiers several Gutenberg Bibles as having been hand copied. Fust's ruse didn't just fail. It so raised the ire of church scribes that they damned printing as a "black art" practiced by the devil.

Also, the similarity of names—Fust and Faust—led some to connect Gutenberg's partner with the German classic's protagonist who makes a pact with the devil.

"Demon" letters

In your youth, you may have been admonished to *"mind your p's and q's."* Some attribute this expression to a barkeeper's pints and quarts, but to printers, the warning referred to letters that they found difficult to distinguish.

Letters easily confused included lowercase ones like *p, q, b,* and *d* as well as capital O and numeral zero. They became "demon" letters—another black-art link to print.

Some dark sides of the "Divine Art"

Print's blessings would prove to be mixed:

- On the religious front, it may have fostered the religious wars of the sixteenth century.
- Because it threatened to obviate the need to master mnemonics, Spanish poet Jorge Manrique (c. 1440–1479) decried the coming of printed books, echoing ancient Greek intellects who scorned the scribal alphabet.
- For good or evil, printing opened the way for many to substitute ideals more concerned with work and prosperity for the ideals based on prayer and salvation.
- The shift from script to print minimized the need for such mnemonic tools as cadence, rhyme, images, and icons that had helped preserve the collective memory since antiquity.

Other craftsmen improved Gutenberg's invention, and by 1500, it had evolved into the process that would remain virtually unchanged for almost four centuries.

The knowledge-sharing power of his invention nurtured the demise of feudalism in Western Europe and caused the Catholic Church—the most powerful institution in the world for a thousand years—to begin to tremble and crumble.

When *TIME* magazine named Gutenberg its man of the last millennium, its cover article concluded, "Most important of all, printing proved to be *the greatest extension of human consciousness ever created.*"

Ben Franklin, printer

His printer's pride led him to write his epitaph focused on his trade.

Printers Spur Rise of Democracies[16]

Printers' roles in the rise of democracies were so manifold that to detail them would fill volumes.

Suffice it here to single out two famous Americans, Thomas Jefferson for his belief in print power, and Benjamin Franklin for his printer pride.

As president, Jefferson cited democracy's debt to the preservative powers of print.

Principal author of the Declaration of Independence, he stressed that instead of documents being so precious that they had to be put under lock and key, printing let them be removed from chests and vaults and duplicated for all to see.

Franklin, according to Time magazine, was the most remarkable of this nation's founding fathers. He succeeded as author, satirist, politician, scientist, inventor, civic activist, statesman and diplomat.

Franklin, nevertheless, in an epitaph of his own composition focused on his first trade thusly:

B. Franklin, Printer.
Like the Cover of an Old Book
Its Contents torn Out
And Stript of its Lettering and Gilding.

Ben Franklin wrote—not with a pen—but with alphabetic metal characters. So he updated the ancient "pen is mightier than the sword" proverb with this revision to make it fit his times:

"Give me 26 soldiers of lead, and I will conquer the world."

Customers of Franklin's and similar small print shops included "pamphleteers"—common citizens who could afford to hurl their ideas into a democracy's political ring.

Flexible in size, pamphlets could communicate expressions ranging from brief exchanges of opposing thought to more serious pronouncements upon questions of the day. Some of the writings were outrageous, defamatory or even seditious; others serious, thought provoking, or even scholarly.

---

16 Search Google images for "Ben Franklin, Printer" and Wikipedia for "Ben Franklin"

CHAPTER 15

*Quite simply, Gutenberg's invention burst
open the door to industrial capitalism.*

Capitalism's Link to Ink

Printing's other historic roles tend to obscure its huge impact upon the processes of production and distribution of goods and services.

Consider just a few seldom-mentioned print innovations that helped push open the door to industrial capitalism:

- First example of "mass production."
- First use of metallurgy for production purposes other than jewelry, agriculture, or arms and armor.
- First use of "interchangeable parts," something the rest of the world would not figure out for more than three centuries.

Professor Hart also asserts that Gutenberg pioneered mass production long before the era of waterpower and steam usually associated with the start of the Industrial Revolution.

He contends that the "Literacy Revolution" engendered by Gutenberg's typography gave birth to a "middle class," something far different from the "bourgeois mercantile class" that had always existed. Besides the profit motive, printing offered the chance to become self-educated."

Operation of a Gutenberg press, moreover, involved team effort, including "all the steps from the stack of blank pages to the stack of the printed pages."

One person would bring paper to the press while another prepared the opening of the type bay and still another did the inking. Then the paper was placed in the type bay, pressed against the inked type. Finally it was lifted off and run through the drying process.

"In an emergency situation," Hart grants, "one person could operate a press to a functional degree, but in the usual process a team of printers—not terribly skilled except for the main operator—formed what in modern parlance we call 'the Assembly Line.'"

Yet Hart finds no one crediting Gutenberg for that or for "mass production."

Agents of change to capitalism?

I'd been delving into printing's historic role as an agent of change for decades before I came across the suggestion that pioneer printers initiated modern capitalism. The closer I examined that idea, the more sense it made.

Less than three decades after the completion of Gutenberg's 42-line Bible, to hand set the type for each page of a copy of Plato's *Dialogue* still cost three times what a scribe would charge to hand-script it.

But each page of script cost well over a hundred times the cost per page of a thousand printed off a single typeset page.

Hypothetical example:
- Typeset one page: $3.00
  - o   Print 1,000 pages = $6.33
- Script one page: $1
  - o   Script 1,000 pages = $1,000.00

Gutenberg's typography must have been the first system to gain accuracy and lower costs with a mechanical device that replaced direct handwork.

Interchangeable parts and capitalist profits

Gutenberg standardized interchangeable typefaces more than three centuries before those "revolutionary innovations" of Honoré Blanc and Eli Whitney. It wasn't until the 1780s that Frenchmen in Blanc's workshop turned out metal musket parts on a machine. Whitney didn't win his legendary patent for interchangeable gun parts until 1794.

Print shops also pioneered the revolutionary use of machinery to maximize employee productivity.

In that same capitalistic vein, printed books in the early 1500s empowered a rapidly rising mercantile class by widely disseminating the secrets of double-entry bookkeeping.[17]

In editing and publishing such texts, moreover, printers passed on to others the lessons they had to learn themselves to prosper.

Making no mention that God might disapprove or that 15 percent interest doubles in five years, lessons in books of math instruction explained how to figure exorbitant interest rates and to calculate large profits. In so doing, they undermined church teachings against sharp dealing and usury.

Taking prayer book production out of the hands of the clergy tended to downgrade prayers and monkish ideals while it enhanced the concepts of more worldly hard work and utilitarian values.

Theologians and scholars, many of them monks, became immersed in a new culture of capitalism when they took their texts to print shops. Meanwhile, printers' connection with the "divine art" helped them escape the low social status traditionally assigned to the mercenary trade.

Fonts more expensive than the press

To understand how one might assert that Gutenberg sired industrial capitalism, consider what operating a print shop entailed. The owner had to do the following:

- Make a major investment of about £200[18] in machinery, with the fonts of type costing more than a new press.
- Sell bills of sale, contract forms, deeds, wills, etc. as well as Bibles and other books to recoup investments and make a profit.

Printed papal indulgences (the forgiveness of sins) provided the church with such a profitable source of financing that selling them was said to be "almost like printing money."

---

17 This was too late, of course, for Gutenberg, whose personal bankruptcy spotlighted the dark side of industrial capitalism.

18 Such an investment represented five years earnings for an average craftsman.

Challenging the practice, Luther insisted, "Forgiveness was God's alone to grant," so indulgences could neither absolve buyers from all punishments nor grant them salvation.

Men of letters and business
Pioneer print shop owners doubled as men of letters and men of business. They took on worries and tasks unknown in the age of script. Others besides those mentioned above included:

- Production decisions, such as the size of press runs.
- Distribution and disposal of unsold copies.
- Targeting separate markets, such as academic, church, legal, or erotic.
- Deciding when and where to purchase capital equipment, paper, and ink.
- Financial decisions regarding price setting, loans, payroll, rent, etc.
- Competition from rival profit-driven firms.
- Idle machine time.
- Striking workmen.
- Commercial advertising.

Among the more subjective new decisions print shop owners faced was how to reward authors and editors for their time and skills.

Printers became "carriers of a spirit of capitalism" simply because they were capitalists themselves. The very act of printing Bibles intruded capitalistic enterprise into consecrated space.

When Luther called printing's role "God's highest act of Grace," he lent dignity not just to the print business but also to commerce and trade in general.

CHAPTER 16

The Avon to the Severn runs,
the Severn, to the sea,
and Wickliffe's dust shall spread abroad
wide as the waters be.
—Daniel Webster (1782–1852),
quoted in an address before the Sons of New Hampshire

Shaping the English Language

From near obscurity in the plague-stricken fourteenth century, the English language surged rapidly during the middle of the last millennium to become a powerful Information Technology.

It watered the soil of Western democracy.

Bloody revolts against nobility and the church, furtive translations of the Bible into the vernacular, and the burnings of hundreds of martyrs at the stake played key roles as a riveting drama unfolded.

Main characters included a wealthy merchant-diplomat who turned pioneer printer, two defiant clergy, and Henry VIII with his mistress-wife Anne Boleyn.

"Black Plague" set stage for Peasants Revolt

The Black Death—which had provided a surplus of cheap rags to feed inexpensive paper to pioneer printing shops—created a shortage of peasant labor.

That starved the feudal system into dissolution.

Historians estimate that the pre-plague population in England in 1300 ranged from four to seven million people. Post-plague population estimates drop to as low as two million.

The plague made labor so scarce that many peasants felt free to search for better working conditions. That set the stage for soaring inflation and widespread revolts against feudalism's hierarchal authority.

Parliament reacted to the 1381 Peasants Revolt by levying a new poll tax and imposing wage controls (but no price controls). When the protesting rebels invaded London and caused havoc, King Richard met with them and offered to abolish serfdom, but after the rebels withdrew, the king took back his offer. Hundreds were tried and executed.

For well over a millennium, the Roman Catholic Church had cast itself in the role of the sole proper authority to interpret the Bible, the text of which was available only in Latin. The church held that Christ had given the scriptures to the clergy to preach to the laity and to weaker persons.

Bible reading, even among the clergy, was rare. Most priests mastered little more than the Ten Commandments, the Paternoster ("Our father, who art …"), the Creed, and Ave Maria ("Hail Mary!"). Clergy seldom preached from the scriptures, if they preached at all.

By the fourteenth century, a patriotic desire for a complete national Bible had arisen.

"Poor priests" followed Wycliffe

Foremost among early reformers was John Wycliffe (1330–84). None of his peers matched his insistence on the authority of the Bible.

Wycliffe believed that political power would (and should) ultimately rest with the people. Nevertheless, he believed they needed "to know God's law" before they came into control.

After a stroke partially paralyzed Wycliffe in 1382, some of his other views were declared heretical. He died two years later.

His followers, the Lollards, encountered varying degrees of acceptance, but by 1400, they were at constant risk of their lives. So they hid in deep forests, dells, and mountains and trekked from town to town, receiving food and shelter from their congregations. Their preaching corralled converts all over England.

In 1413, however, the execution of a British lord sympathetic to their cause so frightened the Lollards' upper-class supporters that they deserted the cause. Deprived of their protection, the Lollards had to go even deeper into hiding.

The "Morning Star" of the Reformation

In 1428, the pope ordered Wycliffe's remains disinterred and burned on a bridge over the river Swift, an Avon tributary, and his ashes cast into the stream.

Hence, the following the prophecy:

> *The Avon to the Severn runs,*
> *The Severn to the sea.*
> *And Wycliffe's dust shall spread abroad*
> *Wide as the waters be.*

True to the prophecy, Wycliffe's impact survived his demise. The moving force behind the first translation of the Bible into English, he became the "Morning Star" of the Reformation.

Martyrs' blood christened newer translations because the church feared the following:

- People who could read the Bible in their own tongue would recognize the contradictions between what God's Word said and what the priests taught.
- The church's income and power would crumble.
- No longer would the church be able to sell indulgences (the forgiveness of sins) or sell the release of loved ones from a church-manufactured "purgatory."
- Salvation through faith, not works or donations, would be understood.

William Caxton—merchant, then printer

William Caxton (1422?–1492?) was merchant, diplomat, translator, writer, and printer successively—and successfully in each case. That striking resume fails to reveal the man's historic importance.

Caxton may have done more than anyone, except perhaps Shakespeare, to shape the English language into the powerful Information Technology it's become today.

Apprenticed in his teens to a wealthy London cloth merchant, Caxton quickly mastered the trade. Fluent in French and Latin as well as his native English while still in his early twenties, he moved across the channel to start his own business in Belgium.

In his thirties, when Gutenberg printed his 42-line Bible, Caxton had already prospered trading in the famous Bruges wool market and had been involved in a number of diplomatic missions for England's King Edward IV.

In his mid-forties, he left the wool market to enter the household of Margaret of York, the king's sister and the duchess of Burgundy. With her as his patron, Caxton translated his own copy of *The Recuyell of the Historyes of Troy* from French into English. The book in manuscript was much sought after in England, but the labor of copying was too heavy and too slow to meet the demand.

Opens England's first print shop

So Caxton, now fifty and wealthy, went to Cologne. There, he paid to have a printer teach him the secrets of printing and, in 1474, published the history of Troy that he had translated earlier. The first book to be printed in the English language, its reception was so flattering that he returned to England to set up his own printing shop in 1476 and devoted his remaining years to literature and printing.

His Westminster Press produced England's first known piece of printing—a letter of indulgence. A total of ninety-six carefully crafted and meticulously edited books came off Caxton's press. They included Chaucer's *Canterbury Tales* and Sir Thomas Mallory's *Morte de Arthur*.

The first "creative publisher," Caxton is credited by one biographer with having rewritten—and in so doing, greatly improved—the narratives that had come to him from the Mallory's pen.

Caxton's *The Chronicles of England*, the first English history ever printed, generated "the germs of that opinion which ... made Henry V the national hero and the struggle of Lancaster and York the theme of a national cycle of tragedies," according to noted British scholar C. L. Kingsford.

Caxton blended many dialects into English

Caxton's work as writer and translator merged a wide variety of British dialects, grammars, and spellings into a single literary language—still flexible but widely recognized as English throughout the Western world.

Before Caxton, English had been in flux for centuries. He and his fellow pioneer British printers stabilized the island's language. By the end of sixteenth century it had evolved into modern English.

Caxton died in Westminster in 1492, the same year Columbus made his first voyage to America. Leading scholars have seen fit to credit Caxton with the title of "the father of English literature."[19]

William Tyndale answers need for new Bible

By the mid-1500s Wycliffe's English had become so outmoded—certainly Caxton's doings to some degree—that a need arose for a new Bible easy for everyone to read.

William Tyndale was the first man to print the New Testament in English. A sixteenth-century Protestant reformer, he was so fluent in eight languages that any one of them might have been his native tongue.

Many of the phrases Tyndale coined remain part of our language today, and he's more frequently labeled the "Architect of the English Language" than is William Shakespeare.

Tyndale preached and studied in London for some time before he left England under a pseudonym. After his New Testament translation was printed in 1525 in Worms and Antwerp, copies of it were smuggled into England and Scotland, but the book was condemned the next year.

---

19 When a BBC radio show asked listeners to choose "the British Person of the Millennium," William Shakespeare's 11,717 votes edged out Winston Churchill's 10,957. William Caxton drew 7,108 votes; Charles Darwin, 6,337; Isaac Newton, 4.664; and Oliver Cromwell, 4,653.

"Oh Lord, open the King's eyes"

Its publication led Cardinal Wolsey to condemn Tyndale as a heretic and demand his arrest, so Tyndale went into hiding to revise his New Testament.

Freedom-loving Englishmen drew courage from Tyndale's flight and took delivery of his Bibles hidden in bales of cotton and sacks of flour. The king's men would buy up every copy available to burn them, but then Tyndale would use proceeds from those royal purchases to fund printings to replace them.

In the end—betrayed by an Englishman he had befriended—Tyndale was caught and then incarcerated for five hundred days before he was strangled and burned at the stake in 1536.

Tyndale's last words were, "Oh Lord, open the King of England's eyes."

This prayer would be answered just three years after his martyrdom.

Mistress>wife introduced king to Tyndale

King Henry VIII (1491–1547) was a contemporary of Martin Luther (1483–1546). The king requested that the pope permit him to divorce his wife, who had failed to produce a male heir, and let him marry his mistress, Anne Boleyn.

Anne had strong opinions about religion. She introduced the king to the books of Protestant writers, such as William Tyndale, and tried to persuade him to let Bibles be published in English.

When the pope refused to sanction this marriage, King Henry:

- Married his mistress anyway,
- Denounced Roman Catholicism and took England out from under Rome's religious control, and
- Declared himself reigning head of state and the head of a new church.[20]

---

20 Neither Roman Catholic nor truly Protestant, it became known as the Anglican Church or the Church of England.

King Henry's s first act as "pope" was to order and then fund the first printed English Bible authorized for public use. (Just for spite or at his new queen's[21] urging?)

Over fourteen inches tall, it became known as the "Great Bible" and was distributed to every church and chained to their pulpits. In addition, the new Anglican Church assigned readers to read the word of God to the illiterate so they might hear the scriptures in plain English.

English continued to evolve in both simplicity and flexibility for more than a century after Caxton. The language fully ripened with the publication in 1611 of the *King James Version of the Bible.*

Most literate people recognize the King James Bible's excellence and know that 54 scholars collaborated in its translation. Not nearly so well known are those aforementioned centuries of struggles and sacrifices that led to its creation.

Sun never set on English-speaking British Empire

Before the Norman Conquest of England in 1066, fewer than a million and a half persons on this planet spoke the English language.

In the 1580s, just before the English destroyed the Spanish Armada, Spaniards proudly proclaimed: *"El sol nunca fija en el Imperio Español."*

By the nineteenth century—despite having lost thirteen American colonies—the English paraphrased that phrase to boast proudly: *"The sun never sets on the British Empire."*

After both World War I and World War II, occupation troops of America and its English-speaking allies carried the treasure of our tongue to almost every nook and corner of the earth. American movies have followed suit for almost a century.

Today, Britain no longer rules the seas. Fewer than four hundred million claim English as their first language. That total is less than half the total for Mandarin Chinese and about equal to the numbers of native speakers of Spanish and Hindustan.

---

21 Queen Anne Boleyn's personal copy of Tyndale's 1534 New Testament is displayed at the British Museum.

Yet many believe that the number of native and non-native speakers of English tops the similar total of any other language, and today's increasingly global world relies on English as its primary language for international communications.

A myriad of reasons have been put forth to explain why English came to its planetary dominance. Among them include its directness, its brevity, its diversity, and its lexicon of more than half a million words.

Water for the seeds of American Revolution

History has shown, moreover, that—perhaps by conveying such delicate shades of meaning—English encouraged the sharing of knowledge in a manner conducive to the success of democracies.

The Treasure of Our Tongue drizzled mists of free speech and free thought that swirled into rain clouds of democratic ideals.

They would water the seeds of the American Revolution and spread democracy around the globe.

CHAPTER 17

Mark Twain went bankrupt backing the competitor
of the immigrant watchmaker's Linotype.

Ottmar Mergenthaler Does It Again

Few twentieth-century Americans were aware of —or appreciated— what a wondrous Information Technology made their daily and weekly newspapers, magazines, and books so affordable.

It was Ottmar Mergenthaler's Linotype that had mechanized and outmoded Gutenberg's labor-intensive typography system near the end of the nineteenth century. That invention's revolutionary impact was huge and lasted almost a century, but its inventor's name remained hidden behind the shadows of history.

Ottmar Mergenthaler, nevertheless, deserves a place alongside the likes of other mechanical geniuses, such as Eli Whitney, Alexander Graham Bell, and Thomas Edison.

America in the late nineteenth century

Almost half of this nation's labor force in the early 1880s worked on farms, but a new era of machinery and scientific discovery was bringing drastic changes to the American scene.

Railways and steamships shrank distances, and machinery superseded hand labor everywhere. Revolutionary technologies, such as camera, telegraph, telephone, and typewriter, expedited the gathering and reporting of news. Newspapers circulated into most homes, but none offered more than eight pages.

Books remained almost as expensive—and as rare—as they had been during Abraham Lincoln's youth when he had to walk miles to borrow books from his distant neighbors' small but prized libraries.

Little had changed after more than four centuries. Gutenberg's typesetting process still prevailed. Setting type manually remained extremely labor-intensive.

To create lines of type, a printer still picked letters—one at a time—out of UPPER and lower cases, clicked them into his printer's stick, and then inserted space bands between groups of letters to create words.

He had to justify each line with smaller space bands so that it filled exactly the allotted space between column margins,

Once type had been printed, a "printer's devil"—as young print shop helpers were still known before the advent of union apprentices—randomly and appropriately tossed it into a "hell box."

Later, the printer's devil had to pick out those type characters one-by-one, identify each as to font, size, and style, and return them to their alphabetical UPPER or lower type case boxes.

Inventors had been striving unsuccessfully since the early 1800s to mechanize Gutenberg's labor-intensive process with a machine that would let its operator do the following:

- Gather metal letter molds into words.
- Justify those words in even lines.
- Cast those lines in metal for printing.

Finally, it had to duplicate the printer's-devil job and redistribute the molds so they could be retrieved easily for future printing jobs.

Enter boy wonder Ottmar Mergenthaler

Son of a poor village teacher, Ottmar Mergenthaler was born May 11, 1854, in Germany about a hundred miles southeast of Mainz. That was the same town in which Gutenberg had printed his historic 42-line Bible almost four centuries earlier.

In Ottmar's youth, the clock in his village's Lutheran church bell tower had stood still for years. No clock maker had been able to repair it. One evening, however, its bells rang at evensong.

Soon, the village was abuzz with the news: "The schoolmaster's boy has done it."

When he became fourteen, this precocious boy wanted to study engineering, but his father could not afford to send him to a university. Instead, Ottmar was apprenticed to his step-uncle Louis Hahl, a watchmaker. Before Ottmar finished his apprenticeship, Hahl helped the youth escape conscription into the German Army by paying his steerage passage to America.

The handsome seventeen-year-old carried only a wooden suitcase carved by peasant neighbors when he arrived in Washington, DC, to work in his step-cousin's precision machine shop. When this cousin, August Hahl, moved his business to Baltimore, Ottmar followed. There, he displayed such exceptional skills while he was making working models from inventors' blueprints that August soon took him on as a co-owner entitled to a share of the new shop's profits.

In 1873, Mergenthaler helped several Washington court reporters in their attempt to mechanize typesetting. Their effort failed, but the idea of perfecting such an invention so intrigued him that he made it his life's goal—one that would prove so elusive that patents would be issued for more than a hundred typesetting machines other than his.

In 1876, the holder of one of those patents, Charles Moore, came to the Baltimore shop, seeking Mergenthaler's help. Moore held a patent on a typewriter for newspapers that was designed to eliminate typesetting by hand. It didn't work, so he hired Mergenthaler to try to construct a better model.

Mergenthaler worked for two years with Moore's design and developed a machine that stamped letters and words on cardboard. That effort fell short, but it reinforced Ottmar's belief that huge rewards would follow if he could develop a practical typesetting machine.

Mergenthaler became a US citizen in 1878. That same year, he opened his own shop to concentrate all his efforts on his own typesetting machine ideas.

A terrible fire one night destroyed Mergenthaler's shop, including all his designs and models. Nevertheless, the twenty-three-year-old remained undaunted, because "at home we had no money for school books." He kept trying to develop a machine that would mean "more books—more education for all."

Whitelaw Reid and Darius Ogden Mills
Soon thereafter, Mergenthaler's need for funds to continue his experiments coincided with *New York Tribune* editor Whitelaw Reid's need to reduce his paper's high labor costs.

Reid, born in 1837 on a farm near Xenia, Ohio, so distinguished himself as a Civil War correspondent that Horace Greeley, legendary editor of the *New York Tribune,* made him his managing editor in 1868. Shortly after Greeley's death four years later, Reid—with his father-in-law's backing—seized both financial and editorial control of the *Tribune.*

Reid's wife, Elizabeth, was one of the two children of multimillionaire Darius Ogden Mills, whose rise to fame and fortune rivaled the best of the Horatio Alger dime-novel tales.

Darius was born September 5, 1825, in Westchester county, NY. His father, a wealthy man whose investments went sour, died while Darius was still in his teens.

Forced to go to work as a bank clerk in New York City, Darius did so well at that job that a cousin in Buffalo hired him as cashier entitled to a percentage of the profits of his bank.

Made a fortune selling to '49er miners
By 1848, he had earned enough to follow two brothers who had answered the lure of California gold. Stranded on the Isthmus on his way west, Darius had to detour around South America to get to California. There, he was so successful selling supplies to gold miners and trading in gold dust that he opened the D.O. Mills Bank in Sacramento in 1850 and later helped organize the Bank of San Francisco. That bank, a profitable business with unlimited credit, boasted a capital of five million dollars when Mills resigned as its president and returned East in 1873.

Just two years later, that same Bank of San Francisco closed its doors with millions in liabilities and only hundred thousand dollars in its vaults. The man who succeeded Mills as bank president had fraudulently decimated the bank's finances and committed suicide when his crime became known. Mills accepted a frantic call to return to the bank. He joined others in raising eight million dollars, reopened the bank, and served as president without pay. Just three years later, Mills felt the bank was firmly reestablished and resigned again.

An admirer reportedly said that Mills "dealt in everything but his principles as a banker."

When he returned to New York, Mills grew his own personal investments to an estimated fifty to sixty million dollars in an era when single-digit millionaires were still a rarity.

In his riveting book *The Paper: The Life and Death of the New York Herald Tribune,* Richard Kluger recounts the saga of Mergenthaler's alliance with Mills' son-in-law Whitelaw Reid.

Access to his father-in-law's fortune let Reid make a typesetting machine his first priority. In his vision, it would make printers obsolete. The editor-publisher sent his labor-baiting foreman W. P. Thompson to inspect the contending prototype typesetters. When Thompson returned, he declared that the young machinist Ottmar Mergenthaler had built the best prototype.

In Kluger's account, Reid offered—and Mergenthaler accepted—financial aid along with a thousand shares in the company Reid had organized to create a functional typesetter. Other stockholders included Reid and his father-in-law, whose combined seven thousand shares gave them control of the firm.

Asked himself key question on train

An epiphany reportedly put Mergenthaler on the right track to eventual success. He was riding on a train when these two questions popped into his mind:

- Why a separate machine for casting and another for stamping?
- Why not stamp the letters and immediately cast them in the same machine?

In 1885—fortunately for Mergenthaler and Reid—Linn Boyd Benton patented a punch-cutting machine that could be adapted to cut-type matrixes, molds from which the relief surface of type characters could be cast.[22] Access to affordable matrixes opened the way for Mergenthaler to put the finishing touches on his ingenious invention.

His wondrous machine was ready for its debut at the *New York Tribune* on July 3, 1886. Watching its first successful demonstration, Reid gave the large, clanking machine its name when he exclaimed, "Ottmar, you've done it again! A line o' type!"

Thus was born the Linotype.

Denounced as a "job killer"

Dismayed striking printers who watched Ottmar Mergenthaler turn out the first line-o-type denounced the machine as a "job killer," It did the work of seven men, so printers vigorously opposed its use at the *Tribune*.

Reid became increasingly anti-labor—so angry with the printers' union that a lengthy strike ensued.

Despite early troubles, such as broken and uneven type, just five years after the prototype's introduction at the *Tribune*, a thousand Linotypes had been installed nationwide.

The labor union's war with the *Tribune* lasted six years, ending when Reid accepted a union shop in order to win the 1892 vice-presidential nomination on the Republican ticket headed by Benjamin Harrison. To hold out longer would have jeopardized GOP chances that fall. The anti-labor label, though, did not come unstuck so easily. The Harrison-Reid ticket lost to the Democrats' ticket that Grover Cleveland headed.

Mark Twain backs rival typesetter

In 1889, Mergenthaler produced a faster, almost wear-proof marvel that was succeeded three years later by his Simplex Linotype Model 1 that

---

22 Benton's pantographic punch-cutting machine let a single set of drawings be traced to cut matrices with no need for a punch-cutter's skills. Type design remains a pen and paper profession more than a century later.

became the sensation of the Chicago's Worlds Fair—the Columbian Exposition—in 1893.

Even so, Mergenthaler still faced a potential rival in the Farnham Company that had joined forces in 1877 with James W. Paige, inventor of the Paige Compositor. Farnham's best-known investor was Mark Twain, whose *Tom Sawyer* novel had just been published.

When the company demonstrated Paige's invention for Twain, the famous author harked back two decades to his years as a printer. As had been the case with Ben Franklin, Twain learned the trade as an apprentice to an older brother.

At age twenty-two, before he became a riverboat pilot on the Mississippi, Twain apprenticed at his brother's *Hannibal Journal* and then worked for four years as a journeyman printer in New York City, Philadelphia, St. Louis, and Cincinnati.

Twain, once he'd mastered printing skills, composed his own copy while he was standing before a type case—as could many in the trade. As words came to his mind, rather than writing them first with a pen or pencil, he'd set them directly into type.

Paige's demonstration of his compositor so intrigued the famous author and lecturer that he assumed a major financial responsibility in exchange for a percentage of the anticipated profits.

In designing his machine, however, Paige made two subtle but serious mistakes.

The first was a compulsion to keep improving it. He wasn't ready to patent the production version until 1887. Linotypes had already been on the market for three years, but Paige remained certain he had the better machine. His compositor could set type 60 percent faster than the Linotype. How could he lose!

Paige, however, had designed his machine to function like a human hand's motions. In doing so, his compositor became a temperamental racehorse.

The Linotype, on the other hand, was a steady workhorse that moved in ways humans couldn't. So it was simpler, cheaper, easier to maintain, and less liable to break down. Its tolerances weren't as tight, but Paige's compositor was so much more complicated that it ultimately priced itself right out of the market.

In 1894, about the same time the competitive failure of the compositor became obvious to all, Paige died penniless in a poorhouse.

Twain later repaid all his creditors

Twain had backed Paige's compositor with $300,000[23] even though his publishing house—after its initial success with Gen. Ulysses S. Grant's memoirs—was losing money. Forced into bankruptcy, Twain almost immediately took on a new writing and lecturing workload and voluntarily repaid all his creditors.

The one surviving compositor—a beautiful machine—is housed in the Mark Twain Memorial in Hartford, Connecticut.

Twain later observed that he'd learned two things from the experience: (1) not to invest when you can't afford to and (2) not to invest when you can.

The same year Paige died, Mergenthaler contracted tuberculosis and moved around for several years for treatments but returned to Baltimore in 1897 after a fire destroyed both his New Mexico house and the manuscript of his just-completed autobiography. Ottmar Mergenthaler died less than two years later at age 46. Funeral services were held in Baltimore's Old Zion Lutheran Church. It contains a stained-glass window with a representation of Mergenthaler's Blower, the first model of the Linotype.

23   Equal to $7,518,462 in 2010.

Ottmar Mergenthalter's marvelous Linotype [24]

"Machine-set type was the missing link
in the chain of technological inventions
(such as the rotary press)
that turned printing into one of the earliest
mass-production industries."
— *Richard Kluger*

---

24 Search Google images for "linotype machine" and Wikipedia for "Ottmar Mergenthaler"

CHAPTER 18

This ten-foot-high Rube Goldberg-like contraption may have been history's most complicated and successful invention.

"The Eighth Wonder of the World"

Ottmar Mergenthaler never acquired a title like preeminent inventor Thomas Edison's "The Wizard of Menlo Park," but it was Edison who dubbed Mergenthaler's Linotype "The Eighth Wonder of the World."

A compositor seated at a keyboard took full control of the self-contained factory that lined up character molds into which it squirted hot metal to produce lines of type.

Its keyboard controlled a Rube Goldberg-like contraption that may have been the most complicated and successful invention ever. It was 10-feet high with matrix channels, matrixes of entire fonts of type, belts, wheels, levers, and cams.

Above the keyboard sat the Linotype's magazine—a huge, slotted metal tray that stored thousands of matrixes in different type fonts, styles, and sizes.

Typewritten copy—marked with penciled editing scrawls and ready for typesetting—was clipped to a metal sheet fastened just above the compositor's keyboard.

Alongside the compositor and attached to his machine sat a pot of molten metal (called "lead" by printers, but actually an alloy of lead, antimony, and tin).

After making adjustments for the required column width, font, style, and point size—and with the metal heated to about 550 degrees Fahrenheit—he'd begin setting type. Each of ninety keys controlled a vertical tube filled with matrixes, tiny molds into which an impression of a character had been engraved. Each matrix contained coded notches along its sides that identified the character, font, style, and size of its typeface.

Linotype keyboard keys were split with lower case on the left and UPPER CASE on the right. Responding to a light touch as the compositor's fingers flew, a stream of matrixes—one for each key struck—dropped under the force of gravity into the channels of his machine's magazine and down into a form for a single line of type the width of a newspaper column.

Printer justified lines of type manually

The operator added spaces and hyphens as needed to fill (i.e., justify) each line of text.[25]

Once each line was completed, a bell would ring. The operator pushed the handle to the elevator lever that sent the line of matrixes to the casting form where molten lead that was heated to up to six hundred degrees poured over the matrix molds to form a line of type.

Raised characters in the line of type mirrored the image of the line to be printed. The liquid metal hardened almost instantly and then was discharged onto a metal tray of similar slugs to form a column of type.

(If a slug had been cast without being fully justified, some of the hot metal squeezed through spaces left between loose matrixes and "silver bullets" squirted about ten feet in all directions. So many printers suffered "bullet" burns at one time or another that Linotypes were sometimes disdained as "Magma Dragons.")

Once the line of type had been dropped into the metal tray, pushing another lever elevated the matrixes that molded that line toward the top of the machine until each matrix dropped into its proper storage tube within the Linotype's magazine.

Notches on the sides of matrixes—like those on a key—were coded differently for each character to direct it to its proper storage place in a vertical tube at the top of the machine.

---

25 Your digital word processor automatically does just that if you've clicked onto the "justify" symbol, which sits to the far right of the icons for flush left, center, and flush right.

Lower costs led to more jobs for printers

A skilled compositor working on a Linotype in the English language could set about five lines of type per minute. That was ten times faster than setting type by hand, which took about two minutes to produce one line.

The Linotype also ended the need to sort and return the used type to UPPER and lower cases, where they could immediately be used again. Long aisles of storage cases that had been filled with foundry-produced type became obsolete.

The Linotype cut the costs of most printed materials, not just books. By lowering the labor cost and exploding the market for printed matter, the Linotype in time created many more jobs for printers—NOT fewer.

Its introduction initially displaced thirty-six thousand skilled compositors. But only a decade later, the number of compositors employed equaled the total before the Linotype came into use. That number continued to grow for decades.

Pioneer national printers union was powerful

Ironically, although two compositors were initially thrown out of work for every machine installed, the strength of the International Typographical Union soon enabled the ITU to win major new benefits. The majority of employers in the industry accepted an eight-hour day along with minimum wage standards and a limit on the maximum output per man per day.

The ITU was the oldest national organizer of American labor. No other union managed so quickly and so determinedly to wrest from management so much of its authority over those employed. Newspapers, nevertheless, would reap profits for almost a century that dwarfed those of most industries.

Decades later during the 1930s, historic United Mine Workers (UMW) and United Auto Workers (UAW) strikes and sit-ins merely allowed other unions to catch up with the ITU.

Machine-set type was printing's "missing link"

In *The Paper,* Richard Kluger writes that "machine-set type was the missing link in the chain of technological inventions—such as papermaking machines that ran off continuous rolls and steam-powered rotary presses—that turned printing into one of the earliest mass-production industries."

Along with Mergenthaler's Linotype, these printing developments brought about changes in thought at least as great as had Gutenberg's typography invention.

Lower labor costs spawned penny newspapers and multiplied the total newspaper circulation in this country more than tenfold between 1886 and 1900. It jumped from three million to thirty-three million. Newspapers also became bigger.

Daily editions grew to as many as a hundred pages, and much fatter Sunday editions became the print sensation of the 1890s. Selling advertising earned publishers extraordinary profits that let them sell papers for less than what they cost to produce.

Previously, most journalists had written, edited, and printed each copy of the paper by themselves. Linotypes paved the way for newspapers to recruit full-time reporters to seek out the news. As city populations climbed, the newspapers began reporting everything that happened locally and replaced gossip as the chief source of information about community life.

Opened doors to more educational opportunities

Mergenthaler's invention also opened the door to more educational opportunities than had even been imagined.

Many immigrants learned the English language and how to be "American" primarily by reading those penny newspapers. "He who is without a newspaper," P. T. Barnum declared, "is cut off from his species."

The Linotype made textbooks, such as those that had been handed down as family treasures, so affordable that elementary and high schools as well as colleges and universities could buy them in bulk. (The next chapter will address the Linotype's impact at the beginning of the twentieth century on the explosive growth of public libraries.)

Paraphrasing Elizabeth Eisenstein from her seminal work, the Linotype probably was not the sole agent of change, but it underpinned many of the other agents and engines that shaped the rise of America to world prominence in the twentieth century.

The educational torrent unleashed by the Linotype gained maximum momentum after World War II with passage of the GI Bill of Rights. Its benefits for returning servicemen included an option of full tuition and living expenses for college or vocational school.

That opened the way to higher education for a whole generation of young people, many of whom had never dreamed of going to college before their military service. They, too, benefited greatly from the availability of books and other research materials that the Linotype made affordable.

The Linotype's reign ended short of a full century, but as late as 1980, those wondrous marvels still set 80 percent of the text read around the world.

CHAPTER 19

To enroll women as library students, Melvil Dewey had to overcome vigorous opposition, but his victory opened for them another distinguished field besides nursing and teaching.

Free Self-Learning Laboratories

Few chance connections match the historic coming together that created a revolutionary environment for freely sharing the power of problem-solving knowledge.

In our public libraries near the beginning of the twentieth century, that connection linked the following:

- Ottmar Mergenthaler's 1887 Linotype invention.
- Melvil Dewey's dedication to library science (1875–1925).
- Andrew Carnegie's philanthropy (1901–19).

At home Mergenthaler's family had no money for schoolbooks, and as noted earlier, he thought printing more books might mean "more education for all."

Dewey considered the three great engines of public education to be "church, school, and free public library's good reading."

Carnegie was convinced of—and committed to—the notion that education was life's key.

Modern public libraries slow to evolve

Public libraries date back at least two millennia when scrolls could be read in the dry rooms of public baths in the Roman Empire. Cities in England began opening libraries during the sixteenth-century reign of Henry VIII, and Benjamin Franklin founded America's first circulating library in 1731.

Near the middle of the nineteenth century, some tax-supported libraries in Europe began to lend books and charge no fees unless they became overdue, but the seeds for the modern public library weren't planted until near the start of the twentieth century.

Melville Louis Kossuth Dewey/Melvil Dewey

Wayne A. Weigand's *Irrepressible Reformer: A Biography of Melvil Dewey* describes a convoluted contrarian—one of this nation's most intriguing historic personalities.

Born in 1851 at Adams Center, NY, Melville Louis Kossuth Dewey was the fifth child of religious parents who were respected as the hardest workers in town. As a boy, Melville displayed similar diligence, working after school at his father's boots and shoes store and doing household chores on weekends.

He thought the English language was beautiful but "filled with odd word spellings difficult for non-Anglo-Saxons to master." He suggested, for instance, "sugtons" for "suggestions." He also took an active interest in promoting the metric system and in mastering shorthand.

When he left home for college, he demonstrated his lifetime zeal for reformed spelling. He shortened his birth name, Melville Louis Kossuth Dewey, to Melvil Dui, but he abandoned Dui when his bank refused to honor that signature on a check. He became Melvil Dewey from that time on.

At Amherst College, he began a systematic study of libraries that led to his Dewey Decimal Classification (DDC) system. Interested librarians and professors at Amherst helped him divide the entirety of man's knowledge into ten categories.

Until then, systems had varied , but most libraries arranged books on shelves alphabetically by author or title. That way, books about different subjects wound up jumbled together illogically. (Hardly anything "happens in the real world in alphabetical order," an *Oxford American Dictionary* editor once remarked.)

The DDC established these initial divisions for shelving books:

- (000) Organization of knowledge
- (100) Philosophy
- (200) Theology
- (300) Sociology
- (400) Philology
- (500) Natural Sciences
- (600) Useful Arts
- (700) Fine Arts
- (800) Literature
- (900) History

Divisions were subdivided, first using the second and third digits and then by a decimal point and more numbers. (Note that the sequence recognizes the proper placement of zero by starting with 000 rather than 100.)

Leaves Amherst to "educate masses"

Foreseeing a market for educational tools and for standard forms, Dewey joined partnership with his DDC publisher and quit his Amherst library job to produce and market metric and library devices.

Named chief librarian later at Columbia College, New York, he set up its School of Library Economy—the world's first library science curriculum. Then, despite vigorous opposition, he enrolled women as students.[26]

Melvil Dewey not only developed a method to organize ever-expanding stocks of books so they could be easily accessed. He also added another distinguished field for women by creating a corps of women librarians to circulate those books into the hands of the public and then back onto their places on library shelves.

---

26 Ironically, prominent women in the American Library Association, which Dewey founded, were reportedly ready to resign in 1906 because he violated Victorian standards of social conduct. They accused him of "publicly hugging, squeezing, and kissing several ALA women."

Andrew Carnegie, the man

During Andrew Carnegie's childhood, powered looms outmoded his father's hand-loom weaving trade. The ensuing economic downturn prompted the family to emigrate to the United States.

After the family settled in a Scottish colony near Pittsburgh, twelve-year-old Andrew worked during the day as a cotton-factory bobbin boy monitoring spindles of yarn. Nights, he studied and attended night school.

Colonel James Anderson opened his personal library of four hundred volumes to working boys each Saturday night, and Andrew took full advantage of free access to such a treasure chest of valuable books.

When Andrew became a telegraph messenger, he paid close attention to the instruments in the office, learned to translate Morse code dot-dash clicks, and became a telegraph operator within a year.

His subsequent rise was rapid—first in railroading and eventually in the steel business as a no-holds-barred industrial baron. It culminated in 1901 with the sale of his Carnegie Steel Corporation to J. P. Morgan's newly formed US Steel Corporation.

Carnegie wealth history's second largest

Measuring a person's peak wealth as a percentage of the national economy down through history, only that of John D. Rockefeller exceeded Carnegie's, according to the blog Neatorama.

At the age of thirty-three, more than a half century before his death, Carnegie had written in a memo to himself that "the man who dies … rich dies in disgrace." He believed that "those most anxious and able to help themselves … deserve and will be benefited by help from others."

Convinced that reading was one of the very best ways to learn, he fully recognized the power of access to information.

His "Carnegie Formula" asked municipalities to demonstrate their willingness to support a library by pledging to do the following:

- Donate a site for the building.

- Levy taxes annually to provide 10 percent of the cost of the library's construction to support its operation.
- Provide free library service to all.[27]

The first of Carnegie's public libraries opened in his hometown, Dunfermline, Scotland, in 1883. The locally quarried sandstone building displays at its entrance a stylized sun with a carved motto, "Let there be light."

His first library in the United States was built in 1889 in Braddock, Pennsylvania, home to one of the Carnegie Steel Company's mills.

"Self-Service" stacks revolutionary

Patrons of earlier public libraries had to ask a circulation clerk to retrieve books from closed stacks, but Carnegie libraries introduced a then-revolutionary self-service policy.

Although access to stacks containing reference materials like encyclopedias still was restricted, most stacks were open to the public in nearly all Carnegie libraries. Staff stood ready behind the circulation desk just inside the library entrance to help people find books, but they encouraged the public to browse and discover books on their own.

Carnegie grants and matching local funds financed construction of libraries in forty-seven of the forty-eight states back then, missing only Rhode Island. Almost three out of four were built in small towns with fewer than ten thousand people.

Between 1896 and 1925, the number of these reading laboratories in the United States exploded from about 900 to almost 3,900, nearly half of them Carnegie libraries.

---

27   In the segregated South, where most libraries barred access to "colored," Carnegie bowed to the reality of segregation at that time and funded separate libraries for African-Americans.

Self-teaching laboratories open to all

That Mergenthaler-Dewey-Carnegie trio made these contributions to the creation of wondrous, self-teaching laboratories open to all:

- The Linotype enabled libraries to buy millions of books previously out of their price range and to amass book inventories once unimaginable.
- The Dewey Decimal Classification (DDC) made those huge book inventories manageable and easy to access.
  o DDC cards in catalog drawers enabled patrons to find the specific information they sought and librarians to replace loaned books on their proper shelves where other patrons could find them as needed.
  o By the time of Dewey's death, more than 96 percent of all American libraries still used the DDC system.
- Andrew Carnegie's philanthropy set in motion the building of thousands of modern libraries—so many that public libraries became almost ubiquitous in this nation's towns, villages, towns, and cities.

This InfoTech alliance exploded the sharing of problem-solving knowledge to record levels and gave a powerful thrust to the rise of the United States to world prominence in the twentieth century.

Linotype third leg
of knowledge-sharing
'InfoTech Trinity' [28]

Ottmar Mergenthaler's Linotype
made books affordable
for Andrew Carnegie's
public libraries.

Melvil Dewey's
Decimal Classifications system
made them easy to find
by checking data cards
in catalog drawers.

---

28 Search Google images for "Library catalog drawers" and Wikipedia for
    "Melvil Dewey" and "Andrew Carnegie"

CHAPTER 20

Smoke and the acrid smell of hot lead in the back shop blended with the clickety-clack of a gang of wondrous Linotypes in full cry.

Linotype's Digital Demise

The following *imaginary* visit to a newspaper might best reveal how drastically the digital revolution's sudden arrival in 1980 changed the process of putting out a newspaper.

A visit to a mid-twentieth century newspaper

The tawdriness of the newsroom contrasts sharply with the sterile, early-twenty-first-century cubicle culture. Atop about fifty grey-green steel desks sit upright manual typewriters surrounded by paste pots, ashtrays, oversized scissors, and stacks of copy paper cut from the waste ends of press rolls.

Each desk has a drawer with hanging, letter-size folders on the right side and three small drawers on the left. In those drawers, we might find pencils, pens, notes, files of clippings, matches, and maybe a carton of cigarettes, some cigars, or a whisky flask or two.

A large horseshoe desk dominates the room. From its center the managing editor supervises local and wire news editors stationed inside and outside the rim. Wearing dress shirts but with the top button undone, ties pulled loose and sleeves rolled up, they're a disheveled bunch. Some of the old codgers wear green eyeshades.

An editor pencils editing marks on letter-size sheets pasted together end to end. Finished editing a piece of copy, he typewrites the story's headline and pastes it on top of its paper string. Rolling that all up, he carries it to the wall behind the horseshoe's open end where pneumatic tubes run to and from the composing room. The copy editor picks up one of the empty, foot-long capsules from an open box, jams his paper scroll into the capsule, and shoves it into the outgoing pneumatic tube.

Vacuum swishes it out to the back shop. (In 1949, on the second floor of the Murphysboro Independent, *the copy editor would drop edited copy into an open stovepipe under his desk. The stovepipe emptied into the printers' composing room on the main floor below.)*

A small glassed-in enclosure next to the newsroom houses noisy clattering teletypes. They spit out an endless stream of wire service copy. Ringing bells alert the wire desk to urgent news. "Flashes" read more like headlines. "Bulletins" summarized the story to come in a brief sentence or two.

Copyboys fill paste pots on the desks of reporter and editors and run errands when not hustling reporters' typewritten pages to the city desk in response to cries of "Copy!"

Moving out to the back shop

Upon entering the back shop, the smoke and acrid smell of hot lead meld with the clickety-clack of a gang of wondrous Linotypes in full cry. Journeymen printers' unique cream-white aprons hold type-handling tools—pencils, metal pica rulers, makeup rules, and slug cutters.

Heated vats alongside towering typesetting machines melt twenty-eight-pound lead-and-anatomy cylinders, "pigs" needed to form the type characters.

An operator presses keys on a keyboard divided into banks of upper and lower case characters to turn its wheels, move its metal arms, and drop brass letter matrixes into line. Then he manually inserts space bands to fill out the line before he pulls the lever that pours the molten metal to form the line of type.

When the metal cools, it's called a "slug".

After a slug drops onto a galley, the printer pushes a lever to send the matrixes back to the top of the machine. Coded notches on their sides channel them into their storage spots. Then each matrix sits ready for a keystroke to release it so gravity can pull it back down to join another line of type.

According to back shop mythology, these marvelous machines have ten thousand moving parts!

During their apprenticeships, all printers learn to pick and place individual letters, punctuation marks, and numbers one by one Gutenberg-style into their printer sticks to create headlines or ad lines of large type. Stacks of drawers under heavy stone tops (banks) hold upper and lowercase type fonts from 6 pt. through 96 pt.

Printers place columns of body type within four-sided metal page frames (chases) atop the level banks. Then they insert rules between columns and between handset headlines and the body type to "make up" newspaper pages. Once all the columns have been fitted top, bottom, and sides, the makeup man adjusts screws on the chase to lock the page form tightly before he slides it onto a "turtle," a heavy metal table on rollers exactly the height of the bank, and rolls it to the stereotype department. There, a solid, curved, metal page is cast to be mounted on the rotary press, which spits out tens of thousands of papers an hour.

Computers duplicate printers' skills

In 1980, the *Kalamazoo Gazette* sent me to Ann Arbor to learn how to operate ATEX digital word processors.

The ATEX system transferred the printers' back shop typesetting skills onto computers in the newsroom. It let reporters compose text that editors could edit, format, and send to photocomposition machines that turned out printed copy.

By May 13, 1980, most of the newsroom staff had been trained on the ATEX system, but it had not yet been used to produce the paper. That afternoon's press run had just finished when Kalamazoo's deadliest and most damaging tornado struck. About 5:00 p.m., the publisher called all editors, reporters, and printers back to the newspaper to produce its first extra edition in decades.

From "hot type" to digital instantaneously

That night, the *Gazette* hurtled from the "hot type" era into the digital age.

Earlier that year, a brand new, $40,000 hot-type-setting machine had been set up in the back shop. Barely a year later, the *Gazette* had to pay to have it hauled away as junk.

That memory brings to mind the following quote from someone whose name escapes me:

"By the time you can buy the latest technology and get it running in any kind of optimized manner, it's obsolete!"

Digital software let editors duplicate printer tasks on their keyboards, choose type fonts and sizes, select bold, italic, or underlined, set it flush left, center, flush right, or justified, and perform other typographic functions.

Their hard-earned skills no longer needed, "hot type" printers with their unique aprons and tools disappeared from the back shop forever, as did the Linotypes except for one labeled museum piece that sits in the paper's public entrance lobby.

One *Gazette* printer immediately enrolled in a computer course at Kalamazoo Valley Community College. There, he digitalized his printer skills so quickly that he taught word processing on PCs as a member of the KVCC faculty the next year.

By 1986, the year I retired, putting out the paper was neither tawdry nor romantic. The newsroom resembled a sterile business office. Typing, cutting, copying, and pasting remained there as computer keystrokes, but copyboys, messy paste pots, clattering teletypes, electric typewriters, long scissors, or swooshing pneumatic tubes were gone.

"ETAION SHRDLU"

This absurd phrase —"etaion shrdlu"— may seem absurd and unintelligible, but it brings to my mind many fond memories of back shop lore. For instance:

- Hellbox, which held type to be melted down,
- Pica pole, a printer's ruler marked in picas, inches and agate lines;
- Pi, as a noun — a mass of dumped type, or as a verb — to dump type.

But back to "etaion shrdlu." Those two nonsensical groupings of letters represent the approximate frequency of the 12 most commonly used English letters.

They filled the first two vertical columns on the left side of Linotype keyboards.

When an operator discovered in the middle of setting a line that he'd made an error, he'd fill out that line by drawing his index finger down the first row of keys — e-t-a-i-o-n. Next, he'd swipe the second row — s-h-r-l-d-u.

The resulting phrase was so distinctive that it usually caught the eye of either the Linotype operator or the proofreader and was discarded. On rare occasions, however, it slipped into print and puzzled newspaper readers.[29]

In letters to the editor they used to ask, "Just what is this etaion shrdlu?

The last issue of the New York *Times* printed before the switch to the digital cold-type process carried a documentary titled *"Farewell, Etaoin Shrdlu."*

---

29 This happened often enough for ETAOIN SHRDLU to be listed in the Oxford English Dictionary and in the Random House Webster's Unabridged Dictionary.

CHAPTER 21

"Einstein wasn't very good at math."
—John Kemeny (1926–92), BASIC author

The Seeds of Cyberspace

Back in the middle of the eighteenth century, Benjamin Franklin pointed the way to the *Age of Cyberspace*. Whether or not he actually flew his kite in a thunderstorm, this one-time printer-by-trade was the first to focus public attention on the potential of electricity as a positive force of nature.

Franklin's lightning rod also arguably pioneered putting knowledge of electricity to practical use.

Before moving on to the marvels Franklin would spark, let's take a brief side trip along the InfoTech trail. Two mundane tools escaped mention until now despite their significant contributions to the creation of information technologies and the sharing of the power of knowledge.

Pencils and blackboard chalk
The first is the pencil. Henry Petroski grabbed me with one engaging tale after another through 340 pages in his book, *The Pencil*. It had never occurred to me, but common sense confirms his contention that with engineers and architects "everything begins with a pencil."

Petroski traces the pencils origin back to ancient times and then cites its reincarnation with the discovery of graphite in England in the sixteenth century. He considers the pencil not just the tool of engineers but perhaps the ultimate example of engineering itself. [30]

---

30 To finance his writing by Walden Pond, Henry David Thoreau worked as a surveyor and in his family's pencil and graphite-processing business. There, he devised a mix of clay and inferior graphite that produced a smear-free pencil with controllable hardness.

The pencil managed to survive against such formidable competitors as the pen and remained the workhorse of composition and calculation from kindergarten on to higher grades through most of the twentieth century.

Ubiquitous chalk teaching tools

Chalk coupled with chalkboard makes up our second useful but mundane tool.

As was the case with pencils, the sticks of calcium sulphate we called chalk were ubiquitous in classrooms I frequented from kindergarten through college.

Like pencil and paper, chalk and chalkboards—we called them blackboards—deserve education's highest honorariums as teacher tools. Photos of chalk-wielding Albert Einstein testify to how indispensable they became even at the highest levels of science.

Electronic InfoTech's path to Cyberspace

Now, let's turn back to the fruits of Ben Franklin's kite flying.

Not until the nineteenth century did a host of inventors set in motion the development of devices using electrical power that belong in any listing of Information Technologies.

Each one greatly accelerated the sharing of knowledge, but history is rather hazy about who deserves credit for many of them.

Among the most famous Europeans and Americans were Guglielmo Marconi, Nikola Tesla, Thomas Edison, Alexander Graham Bell, Thomas Watson, Lee DeForest, William S. Paley, and Philo Farnsworth.

Equally hazy are which dates most deserve consideration as the birth of these inventions. Most had gestation periods that stretched over a number of years.

Electronic InfoTech chronologically

1830s and '40s
- Wired telegraph
  - Developed separately in England and the United States, it crystallized on May 24, 1844, with Samuel Morse's "What hath God wrought?" (Numbers 23:23) message.

1876
- Telephone
  o Who doesn't recall learning of Bell's peremptory "Watson, come here. I want you!"

1877
- Phonograph

1879
- Lightbulb

1880
- Electricity distribution

1906–1919
- Radio

1920s
- Television

1930s (or sooner)
- Punch cards to input and externally store data

The final seeds of Cyberspace, however, weren't planted until 1939 when US Army Ordnance scientists built the world's first electronic computer to calculate ballistic firing tables that would be used in World War II.

Those seeds rapidly took root, sprouted, and continue to send out new growth.

More Electronic InfoTech chronologically

1940s
- First digital programmable electronic computer. (Digital computers typically use just two voltage levels: 0 for OFF and 1 for ON. Previously, analog computers, which represented data with variable voltages, had been the world's most powerful.)

1946
- The Electronic Numerical Integrator and Computer (ENIAC). Built at the University of Pennsylvania's School of Engineering, it was the prototype from which most other modern computers evolved. A grotesque thirty-ton monster with 19,000 vacuum

tubes instead of microchips, it incorporated almost everything found in today's high-speed computers.

1950s

- Rotating magnetic drums for internal storage of data and programs.
- Transistors replace vacuum tubes.

1952

- *Pre-election polls predicted a close contest between Illinois Gov. Adlai Stevenson and five-star Gen. Dwight D. Eisenhower. Early election night, the ENIAC predicted a landslide victory for the GOP's general, but the news media—certain that ENIAC had blundered—censored that accurate call until morning vote totals had confirmed it.*

1960s

- Integrated circuits replace transistors.
- Plain-paper copying machine.

1969

- Seeds planted for the Internet.
- Less technical computer languages like BASIC.

1970s

- CPUs, e-mail, and PCs on a single chip (Apple II, Macintosh, Motorola).

1980s

- The Internet is in full bloom.
- IBM PC with MS-DOS, Windows, laptops.
- World Wide Web, cellular phones.

1990s

- Wireless networking, webcams, GPS, smart phones.

The pioneers

Many creative individuals laid blocks for the latest information technology's foundation, but the above chronology spotlights no single inventor, such as paper's Ts'ai Lun, the print shop's Johann Gutenberg, or the Linotype's Ottmar Mergenthaler.

Some have become celebrities, many millionaires, and a few billionaires. Yet most resemble more closely those who in near-anonymity developed pictograph and phonetic writing systems.

Although others may have been more technology-gifted or become better known to the public, these two pioneers remain my personal InfoTech heroes:

- Vannevar Bush (not related to the presidential family) (1890–1974)
- John Kemeny (1926–92).

Vannevar Bush envisioned a library in a desk

Near the end of World War II, Bush became for many the "sage of Cyberspace."

Born in Everett, Massachusetts, he earned his bachelor's degree at Tufts College in just three years and in 1917 received a joint doctorate in engineering from Massachusetts Institute of Technology and Harvard University.

By 1945, Bush had made an impressive mark in the world:

- Co-founder of Raytheon Corporation, MIT's dean of engineering
- President of the Carnegie Institute of Washington
- A primary organizer of the Manhattan Project that produced the atom bomb

Perhaps of more significance, President Franklin Delano Roosevelt called upon Bush during World War II to mobilize military, industrial, and academic scientists to share their problem-solving knowledge and coordinate wartime research efforts.

In the 1930s, Bush focused on building an analog device he hoped would revolutionize computing. In a 1945 *Atlantic Monthly* article "As We May Think," he described a theoretical machine he called a "memex."

He targeted its microfilm technology to enhance human memory by letting its user store, index, cross-reference, and retrieve documents linked by associations. This associative linking was very similar to what is known today as hypertext.

Envisioned encyclopedia "in a matchbox"

Bush wrote that the *Encyclopedia Britannica* "could be reduced to the volume of a matchbox. A library of a million volumes could be compressed into one end of a desk."

He envisioned being able to assemble, compress, and deliver in a moving van "the total record of everything printed since the invention of movable type."

(That's true already, but more than three decades after Bush wrote that, the ceiling-high computer that ran the *Gazette's* ATEX system filled a whole room.)

Although his years of memex experiments failed to produce a practical working model, his word image of "a library desk" in that *Atlantic* article anticipated just how drastically computers might increase our access to information and consequently alter our future culture in a radical way.

Bush's Internet legacy lists nothing in the way of a machine or digital software. Yet his vision inspired others to carry on the work, and his leadership pulled together universities, the federal government, and the military in a powerful combine that played perhaps the major role in making the concept of Cyberspace a reality.

Internet emerges from the United States reaction to Sputnik

On October 4, 1957, the USSR won the race to outer space with its launch of Sputnik, followed closely by the Soviet's first intercontinental ballistic missile test. President Eisenhower reacted by setting in motion an aggressive military campaign that gave birth to the United States' Advanced Research Projects Agency (ARPA).

In 1958, however, the National Aeronautics and Space Administration (NASA) was formed to direct the government's space and strategic missile research while ARPA turned its focus on computer science and information processing.

In 1959, computers at different American universities began talking to each other on ARPAnet, the world's first multiple-site computer network. This pioneer packet-switching network then evolved into the Internet we know today that connects ground-based, radio, and satellite networks.

In 1974, Vint Cerf ("father of the Internet" to some) and Bob Kahn wrote the Transmission Control Protocol (TCP). That let the various networks connect in a true "Internet." By the 1980s, it connected the computers of most universities and research institutions.

Kemeny helped Albert Einstein with his math

Born in Hungary, John Kemeny came to America in 1940 after his father foresaw the dark future of Jews under the Nazis and brought his family here. A grandfather as well as an aunt and uncle perished in the Holocaust. This prodigy was only thirteen when he learned his first word of English but managed to major in both philosophy and math while he was earning his degree from Princeton in just three years.

While Kemeny worked on the Manhattan Project in Los Alamos, his boss for a year was Nobel Prize-winner Richard Feynman, who had assisted in establishing the system for using IBM punch cards for computation.

Then, as a twenty-two-year-old working on his PhD, Kemeny served as a mathematical assistant to Dr. Albert Einstein. (Asked why the famed physicist needed such an aide, Kemeny explained, "Einstein wasn't very good at math.")

Prior to the 1960s, one had to be able to write custom software in order to use a computer, and very few besides scientists and mathematicians could do so. In 1959, Kemeny and Thomas Eugene Kurtz began looking for a way to provide their Dartmouth College students with the skills needed to do their own computing.

Using a Royal McBee LGP-30 computer, they managed to create a language that outmoded the old computer way of writing similar to how the alphabet antiquated pictograph writing.

Kemeny and Kurtz coupled their Beginner's All-purpose Symbolic Instruction Code (BASIC) with their Dartmouth Time Sharing System

(DTSS) and a GE system to bring DTSS and BASIC to students on the Dartmouth campus in fall 1964.

In the 1970s and 1980s, BASIC and its variants became the computer language of choice on microcomputers, and computing no longer remained the restricted domain of the scientific hierarchy.

Kemeny would serve as president of Dartmouth from 1970 to 1981, during which time he continued to teach undergraduate courses and do research and publish papers. His administration opened Dartmouth's student body to women, ending two centuries of single-sex education, and initiated year-round operations, which allowed the student body to expand without expanding physical facilities.

In 1982, he returned to teaching full-time for another decade.

Then there's Pierre Omidyar.

Perhaps the most intriguing digital InfoTech pioneer is Pierre Omidyar, founder of eBay.

No summary here, however, could do justice to the Adam Cohen's almost perfect story about how altruism prompted Omidyar to build eBay and led him to riches as great as almost any that greed has engendered. Cohen writes it in *The Perfect Store: Inside eBay.*

Like all the other wondrous InfoTech, the Internet with its non-central, nonhierarchical nature has already been historically world changing.

Recalling that more paper books were produced in first fifty years of Gutenberg Press than in all previous history, Professor Hart suggests that there will be more free eBooks created in years up to 2050 than all the paper books printed before 2000.

I'll not try here to keep abreast of (or opine about) twenty-first century InfoTech progress. Having been retired and out of the work world for a quarter century, my knowledge of it probably lags well behind that of most readers.

Ahead, however, lay some thoughts on knowledge-sharing—then and now— followed by Professor Hart's Epilogue.

CHAPTER 22

The world is ruled by force, not by opinion,
but opinion uses force.
—Blaise Pascal (1623–62)

Knowledge-Sharing—Then and Now

The stream of shared access to problem-solving knowledge began with the trickle of Homo sapiens' language and memory. The stream then swelled with each succeeding new Information Iechnology.

By breaking the chains of ignorance for ever-increasing portions of the population, each of those evolutions and revolutions expanded the knowledge base.

Most acted as a powerful agent—but not necessarily the sole agent—that upset the balance of power within a civilization.

First, fully articulated speech let our ancestors share the knowledge needed to control fire and master the tools and weapons that let our species dominate this planet.

Then:

- Writing symbols of shape broke ancient tribal bonds and transferred tribal chief powers to the warrior leaders and priests who built and managed city-states in an agrarian society.
- Wondrous, alphabetic symbols of sound helped Alexander the Great and the Roman Caesars conquer and administer empires that dominated huge areas of the known world in their time.
- Islam resurrected the ancient classics, and both Muslims and Mongols delivered the Chinese paper secret and Hindu mathematics from the Orient to the West.
- By the fourteenth century, China had used paper and block printing for centuries, and its empire boasted city-states with

populations in the millions —so wealthy that Columbus dared sail west into the unknown, hoping to find a sea route to reach them.

Most radical intellectual changes ever

- By bringing about the most radical changes ever in intellectual life, Gutenberg's typography:
  o Tipped the balance of power from feudal royalty toward a middle class of business and industrial leaders.
  o Bolstered the Reformation, the Industrial Revolution, modern science, and democracy.
  o Spurred the rise of the West.
- William Caxton merged a mix mainly of Anglo-Saxon, Norse, and French tongues into an English language that drizzled mists of free speech and free thought that later swirled into rain clouds of democratic ideals.

By fostering major growth in literacy and education at all levels and in scientific research as well, the Mergenthaler-Dewey-Carnegie trio gave a substantial push to the United States' rise to world prominence during the twentieth century.

Looking ahead in the Age of Cyberspace

Rapid as was the surge in access to problem-solving InfoTech during the first half of the last century, the digital torrent unleashed in 1946 by the ENIAC—the prototype of the world's first modern computer—was even more dramatic.

Following the first manned mission to the moon in 1969, we were rapidly introduced to desktop computers, the Internet and the World Wide Web, laptop computers, mobile phones, tablet computers, and digital social networking.

Soon, individuals could transmit not just text and sound but also active visual images—first to other individuals but later to social media sites of every sort.

Back in the twentieth century, revolutionaries first targeted radio stations because they were the primary source of information for the vast majority and almost daily spouted the dictators' propaganda.

Then in the first decade of the twenty-first century:

- **Satellite TV** gave people access on their television sets to real reporting of images and information on CNN, Al Jazeera, Al Arabiya, and other channels that broke state monopolies of information.
- **The Internet** not only provided more information but let the people post information and opinions anonymously on a computer.
- **Social networks** let people share information, opinions, and organizing ideas and helped them organize on their cell phones.

Those successive technologies moved the distribution of information from a one-to-many system to a many-to-many system.

Did InfoTech really upset power balances?

Some readers may decry declarative sentences stating that InfoTech revolutions played major roles in these historic upsets of power balances.

Some of those statements' admittedly subjective bias probably stems from decades trekking the InfoTech trail. Hopefully, skeptics may soften their criticism if they recall the book's aim as stated in its epigraph: *Neither to persuade nor indoctrinate—rather to foster curiosity about past InfoTech.*

Early critics of the Internet and social media raised visions of Web users sitting all alone in the dark staring glassy-eyed at blinking computer screens. Yet we've already witnessed surprising examples of the power social networking can exert.

The Internet showed its political clout as early as the Bill Clinton's 1992 victory over President Bush, not to mention Barack Obama's election in 2008 and the boost it gave to the Tea Party in 2010.

By the beginning of 2011, social bonds forged in Cyberspace had spilled over into turmoil in the Middle East with force strong enough to threaten to overturn the balance of power in more than a dozen Arab nations.

In cases where social media promotes protests aimed at revolution, however, the cart often tends to get ahead of the horse.

InfoTech lets people generate and consolidate discontent with autocratic regimes, but whether protestors can affect a true shift in the balance of power depends upon whether their leaders:

- Clearly state the majority's goals and
- Have prepared to build a governmental structure stable enough to achieve them.

For this latest Information Technology revolution to follow in the path of previous InfoTech, it must continue to enhance sharing problem-solving powers of knowledge and bring about:

- Huge growth in the volume of knowledge readily available, and
- Even greater growth in the share of world population able to access it.

The ease of intercontinental communication
Past InfoTech revolutions and evolutions marched from place to place, transforming cultures in larger and larger regional populations.

The Age of Cyberspace may already have pulled more people from the pool of wasted intellect than did all previous InfoTech. With the growing ease of intercontinental communication, the stream of shared access to problem-solving knowledge rushes around the world.

The twentieth century may have been the Age of America, but China claimed the top spot on the list of the world's supercomputers for its Tianhe-1A by 2010. And in 2011, the International Monetary Fund (IMF) predicted that by 2016 China would overtake the United States as the world's number-one economy.

Whether the first phases of the twenty-first century become the Age of China remains to be seen, but arguably, the trend seems headed toward a Global Age.

Intellectual Property vs. Right to Knowledge

In the past, access to knowledge power did not expand uniformly, and the Age of Cyberspace's sharing of information via satellite points to a new copyright concern.

Opponents of copyright argue that because file sharing can occur when even just one individual sends a file to another, the only way to police copyright infringements is to restrict our right to communicate privately with each other.

Robert B. Laughlin, a Stanford University physics professor, was one of three scientists awarded a 1998 Nobel Prize for discovering a new form of quantum fluid.

His book *The Crime of Reason, And the Closing of the Scientific Mind,* addresses in considerable detail intellectual property rights' pros and cons. It includes this rather harsh criticism of some who defend the concept of intellectual property:

"The right to learn is now aggressively opposed by intellectual property advocates, who want ideas elevated to the status of land, cars, and other physical assets so that their unauthorized acquisition can be prosecuted as theft."

In his Epilogue just ahead in this book, Professor Hart asserts that his studies of copyright tell him that the world's resistance to mass publication of information has been extremely powerful ever since powers of the press began to take over from the scribes and monks by enacting three centuries ago the first of the fully functional copyright laws that still muzzle the Gutenberg Press.

Obviously, proponents of strict copyright laws have prevailed in Congress and the courts, but the public might well benefit by hearing a series of widely publicized debates on a question such as this one:

Resolved: The public good benefits more from moderate copyright laws that encourage freer copying of published works than is now possible under copyright laws lasting for longer than a human lifetime.

Widespread public discussion of the pros and cons of intellectual property hopefully might encourage research aimed at finding ways to avoid (or dismantle) roadblocks that in the past curbed access to expanded knowledge-sharing.

Social Networks and Digital Books Soar

TIME magazine named Facebook founder Mark Zuckerberg its annual "Person of the Year" in 1910 because his social networking system "is transforming the way we live our lives every day."

Facebook surely is doing just that. "Five hundred million" is a blasé figure. But to realize that Facebook's reaching "a half billion people worldwide" is simply startling.

Less noticed have been the rapid growths of both eBooks and Project Gutenberg .

Just as this book's publication deadline neared the Association of American Publishers (AAP) revealed that in February 2011 e-Book sales in the United States were the top selling format in all publishing categories for the first time ever.

Earlier, Professor Hart had sent me a preliminary draft of his 2010 eBook Annual Report that indicated the number of free books distributed online from such sites as Google, Archive.org, Wattpad. com, and Project Gutenberg totaled more than five million.

Facebook and other social networks have pulled the spotlight away from the digitalizing of books phenomenon, but free eBooks seem likely to continue expanding access to problem-solving knowledge far into the future.

Time Line of Information Technology Revolutions

PREHISTORIC
Adam's apple
Hunter-gatherers
Homo sapiens dominates earth

18TH CENTURY BC
Pictograph, logographic, syllabic
First City-States
Mesopotamia, Egypt, China, India

4TH–1ST CENTURIES BC
Phonetics
Greek and Roman empires

1ST CENTURY AD
Invention of paper
China heads toward Golden Age

8TH CENTURY AD
Block printing
Arabs capture papermaking secret

9TH CENTURY
Islamic Golden Age takes root
Carolingian renaissance

13TH CENTURY
Mongols open East-West traffic
Umbilical cord to Western
  Renaissance

14TH CENTURY
China of Marco Polo's Visit

15TH and 16TH CENTURIES
Gutenberg typography
Embryos of Democracy and
  Capitalism
Arabic Numbers and Zero reach West

17TH CENTURY
Caxton standardizes English
King Richard national icon
Sun Never Sets on the British Empire

18TH CENTURY
Democracy blossoms

19TH and 20TH CENTURIES
Linotype and Dewey and Carnegie
Self-teaching laboratories
G.I. Bill of Rights makes college texts
  affordable
US #1 World power

21ST CENTURY
Age of Cyberspace
Digital revolution encompasses globe

Epilogue

By Professor Michael Hart

"No matter how much you push the envelope, it is still stationery."

I use this example to describe my own critical perspective on how copyright keeps stalling the sharing of the written word. My entire life has been one of pushing the envelope and seeing how hard the world pushes back, especially as it has done during the history of eBooks.

The Stationers, from whom we get the term "stationery," [31] started it all, as I'll soon make clear.

The first copyright law

From the Gutenberg Press to steam and electric powered presses, to Xerox copier and the Internet, I have studied the world's resistance to mass publication of information, and a powerful resistance it is. Almost exactly three hundred years ago as I write this, the first copyright law as we know it changed the world by muzzling the Gutenberg Press.

Literally from the day the Gutenberg Press was invented around 1454 the Stationers Guild/Company tried harder and harder to lobby in a law that would outlaw the Gutenberg Press and return their lost publishing monopoly.

That effort finally paid off in 1709 with the adoption of the Statute of Anne 1709–10. Under this law, only twelve printing presses could operate in all of Britain, and they were all in London. If you are a fan of English

---

31   In 1403, text writer and bookseller members of London's first Guild of Stationers worked at fixed positions (stationarius) around the walls of St. Paul's Cathedral.

literature, you probably know just how London's society ran things, and how impossible it was to get anything done if you didn't have the proper London connections.

The new law wiped out the best-laid plans of new reprint houses and left their equipment to be bought at bankruptcy sales by the old boy network of publishers.

If you lived outside London or weren't "connected," this meant that you had little chance of ever being published by "Stationers"—descendants from the long line of scribes down through history—but the Gutenberg Press shattered their long-held script monopolies

The Stationers had struggled for more than a quarter of millennium to recover the loss of their previously unthreatened monopoly of the written word and its publication to the masses.

Lying hidden are tales of "palace intrigue" as well as political machinations, power politics, information manipulation, etc., through the ages. The Stationers' tale—just one of many riveting Information Technology stories hidden in history's shadows—deserves a whole volume of its own.

The Stationers and their descendants stifled numerous "information ages" to keep information from being public, but I'll just list a handful of examples here:

- The Gutenberg Press, stifled by the Statute of Anne, 1709–1710.
- 1830 High Speed Steam Press Patent, stifled by 1831 Copyright Act.
- 1900 High Speed Electric Presses, stifled by1909 US Copyright Act
- 1970 The Xerox Machine, stifled by the 1976 US Copyright Act.
- 1990s The Internet, stifled by the 1998 US Copyright Act.

Each of these five "information age" technologies threatened to do serious damage to the elitist forms of "public-ation" that publishers use to optimize their profits while keeping the public in the dark. In each instance, the power of the government was lobbied in by the publishers to stifle those technologies and to put limits on what might be copied.

We forget sometimes that the term "publication" literally meant "to make public" before the publishing world closed mindedly turned over and over to copyright to create limitations that previously did not exist on the public's legal right to copy. It turns out that it always seems legal to copy as long as the public does not have the means to, but as soon as this changes, new copyright laws should be passed to curtail access via new technologies.

As books get easier and easier to create and take through the publishing process from computer to computer, none of the savings to the publishing industries have been passed on to you, the reader.

Paperbacks cost twenty-five cents at midcentury

In fact, a price comparison from when I first began to buy paperbacks, back around 1955, shows that during pretty much the entire 1940s–1950s the price we paid for a paperback as well as for a gallon of gas averaged about a quarter.

Just twenty-five cents!

Since then we have seen billions of dollars of media coverage about an ever-increasing price of gasoline. But seldom (never?) a single word about book pricing!

In 2010, the average price of a gallon of gas was about $2.50 to $3.00.

That's ten to twelve times as much or 1,000 percent to 1,200 percent inflation.

In 2010, however, the average paperback price was about $10.00.

That's forty times as much inflation or 4,000 percent!

But no one ever mentions that.

In the same vein we must ask, in all honesty, why copyright holders in the United States are the only people who never, ever have to work one more day in their lives to support all their future generations.

It seems most unlikely that Shakespeare collected any royalties. There were, moreover, many great authors who hated copyright. For instance, in his Areopagitica speech—a 1644 prose polemical tract—John Milton urged Parliament to preserve for the English the liberty of unlicensed printing.

Expect another US Copyright Act to be proposed right after or during the 2016 midterm elections.

Yes, copyright has become permanent in the United States as per the 2002 SCOTUS (The Supreme Court of the United States) decision Eldred v. Ashcroft.

The major point here, however, is that publishers control US copyrights, and copyrights will never again expire in the United States without a great change in the public's awareness of this.

This is much more important than it might appear, as we are now at the first point in history where the average person could own a personal library of millions of books and, in 2020, a billion books.

Prices of storage tumble

Right now, today, any computer owner can add terabytes of storage for a small fraction of the computer's price, and each terabyte's ten trillion bytes could hold a million eBooks of a million characters each in plain text format and 2.5 million eBooks in .zip or other compression formats.

Right now, as I write, terabytes are falling to about $50.00. Some copyright experts predict that the copyright laws will simply be overrun in the future by everyone in the world via the Internet and that everyone will have access to copies of everything.

Others say that 99 percent of the people will buy legitimate copies even when free illegal copies are available to all or even when free legal copies are available.

Even though my own efforts through Project Gutenberg have made entire libraries of eBooks available free of charge, some point out that the average person still buys copies of those books rather than use the free ones. So does the average university.

Other copyright experts point out that the US Attorney General's Office, under President Bush II, asked that the copyright infringement penalty be made life imprisonment on top of all the fines we've heard about.

Life in prison for copyright infringement when robbery usually gets only five to ten years?

Here, we get to a historical perspective:

You see, it has always been legal to copy just so long as you couldn't! Before Gutenberg, there were no copyright laws on books or such because none but the most elite knew how to copy them, and none but the richest could afford by a copy made by those elite few.

Laws restrict use of copy technologies

The scribes and monks had a monopoly on writing for all of history right up to that point, and they were terrified at losing that monopoly—and rightfully so.

The Catholic Church, which had been the most powerful institution in the West for a thousand years, declined during the Reformation because of Martin Luther's ninety-five theses meeting with the Gutenberg Press and has never returned to that peak position.

Each time a new technology arrives that could bring an "information age" to the public masses, governments respond by passing laws against copying that stifle the use of that new technology

They have extended copyright forever so we can't read all about it.

You will find that the history of recorded history has been one of the elite, as in "history is written by the winners/conquerors/victors."

Before Gutenberg only about one percent of the people could read or write and preserve their thoughts. A much smaller percentage, moreover, had the power to publish their thoughts, thus leaving the views of the great majority obscured.

After all, 99 percent of all published authors have never written anything on the order of a million books sold and thus don't really communicate along the lines of reaching the entire world. Of course, that is atop quite obvious figures that 99 percent of us are not published authors in the sense—at least what it used to mean before the Internet.

What does this mean in terms of conclusions?

It means that only one person (or less) out of a thousand ever has any voice in setting down the recorded history of the world.

Why not?

Because the powers-that-be don't like to share the power.

The world knows Steve Jobs more because he makes Pixar/Disney movies, not because he invented the PC along with Steve Wozniak. Yet the PC changed the world so much more.

You can be sure this has happened to an even greater degree many times in history, including such inventions as the sewing machine and hundreds or thousands of other inventions.

Restricting the "right" of public domain
Did you know that:

- The public domain is "an inalienable right."
- You can't sell your right to it or buy someone else's right.
- But the government can and does sell your right upstream.

There's a titanic force at work here today. We have this new technology that allows anyone to type or scan any book into a computer and then make it available worldwide in a single day.

Yet copyright laws are now being used to stop all US copyrights from expiring—and those in countries outside the United States as well.

That's what I term "economic warfare."
I can hope that copyright will fail in these objectives, as per:

"There is no force greater than an idea whose time has come."
—Victor Hugo.

"A people cannot hope to be both ignorant and free."
—Thomas Jefferson.

Acknowledgments

I wish to thank Martin M. Cummings, MD, director of the National Library of Medicine (1964–83), for awakening me to the importance of citizen access to knowledge.

Under Dr. Cummings two decades of leadership, the NLM became a unique international force in this computer age—both a major biomedical communications center and one of the most advanced scientific libraries in the world.

This book was barely an embryo—just a jumble of words about past information technologies punched into a computer hard drive—on March 3, 1989, when Dr. Cummings delivered his address on *the Future of the Science Library* at the opening of the University of Florida's Marston Science.

That afternoon when he spoke the following sentence, I jotted it down:

"It is a matter of most importance that our government protect the right of every citizen to have access to knowledge without regard to an individual's ability to pay."

Until the final stages of writing this book, I had stressed that Information Technologies energized the rise of major civilizations without quite understanding how.

Then I came across the above Dr. Cummings quotation I'd written down decades ago.

Suddenly, I realized that Information Technologies expanded the sharing of the power of knowledge and that, in turn, upset the balance of power in one civilization after another.

Recalling Dr. Cummings' words has led me to conclude that the extent and direction of future InfoTech revolutions will probably depend upon how free access to information becomes for the citizens of the world.

Grateful for many different forms of help

To my wife, daughter, son-in-law, and grandson, of course, goes my deepest gratitude for their suffering over decades—both from my ignoring them while my mind wandered and from my episodic rambling and ranting about past and present InfoTech.

I owe Michael Hart sincere thanks, of course—not just for his Foreword and Epilogue but also for his extensive editing and background input on the whole manuscript.

Special thanks go to iUniverse check-in coordinator Nicole Bilby for her patience and professional leadership across the pitfalls of self-publishing and to editorial consultant George Nedeff for his wisdom and willingness to adjust to my sometimes convoluted and unprecedented requests..

Authors in general owe huge debts to library staffs, and I'm no exception.

In the last century, I frequented public and university libraries in Kalamazoo, MI, and Gainesville, FL, to ask their reference desks for help, but the bulk of my queries to librarians have been to Highland Park Public Library staff members under the direction of Jane Conway in the past decade or so. That's when convoluted notes had to be double-checked before they were woven into this text. Julia Johnas, director of adult services, and Barbara Chase on the HPPL reference desk have been especially helpful, as has Cheryl R. Dee, PhD, at the National Library of Medicine.

Author Jack Weatherford was kind enough to grant me free rein in paraphrasing information from his *Genghis Khan* biography. He later confirmed that authorization when I reached him on his cell phone in Mongolia, where he was doing more research last year.

More than a year ago, brother-in-law Dick Wharton earned special thanks for reading manuscript drafts and insisting I'd written a great book. True or not, the praise energized me to continue. Sister Polly Wharton also encouraged me.

Offspring of my wife's sister and their extended families, whom I often bored with my book babbling and who read manuscript chapters, include Katy Kibbey Budzinski, Joe Budzinski, Chris Kibbey, Scott Reetz, Jennifer Kibbey, and Mary and Greg Marr.

At Highland Park High School, I bounced thoughts of past InfoTech off many staffers, including Blake Novotny, Debbie Finn, Gloria Gibson, Suzan Hebson, Luis Vasquez, Barb Harvey, Shannon Bain, Judi Elman, Elizabeth Robertson, and Julie Ann Carroll.

Other Highland Park helpers were Marty Biondi and Jane Ferry from Therapeutic and Wellness and Bill Geraci, my computer guy who staved off computer crashes that threatened to destroy priceless data, and fellow Grand Timers Lynne Samuels and Rollie Reich.

These former colleagues at the *Kalamazoo Gazette* showed interest when I exposed them to my rambling book talk: George Arwady, Bryan Gruley, and Rob Warden.

Other helpers included college classmates Bob McGiffert and Art Morgan, online fellow Cubs fan Hugh Riddle III, Jim M. Rogalski at Duke University Medical Center Public Relations, and Dorothy R. Werner at Princeton's Alumni Association.

Unfortunately, many others have probably been overlooked here, but their input is no less appreciated.

About the Author

A B-29 navigator when he ended three years WWII service in 1946, Brad Bradford returned to Princeton University for his senior year. President of both the University Press Club and the Rugby Club back on campus, he graduated magna cum laude after he wrote his history thesis on the *Birth of the United Nations.*

After two years with United Press, first as a staffer and then managing a small UP bureau, managing editor jobs at small newspapers in Illinois and Montana preceded the start of his thirty-one years at *Kalamazoo Gazette.*

His closest link to modern InfoTech developed after he bought an Apple II computer in 1978. The following year his editor—aware of Brad's new word processing skills— picked him lead the Gazette newsroom into the digital age by doubling as city editor and ATEX computer system leader.

That experience turned Brad's mind both to Gutenberg's historic InfoTech invention and to Otto Mergenthaler's marvelous Linotype printing machines, which he'd admired for three decades. For the ensuing three decades, his hobby has been episodic research for this book.

After he retired in 1986, Brad and his wife, Carol, enjoyed seven years of sun and tennis in Gainesville, FL, where he freelanced an article titled "The Ten Commandments of Tennis Rooting" for *Tennis* magazine.

In 1993, they moved to be near their daughter, Anne, a Bank of America systems analyst who cut her computer teeth as a fourteen-year-old on Brad's Apple II. Her husband Walter Fyk and their son Michael have been especially helpful in steering me away from misinterpreting current trends in the digital world.

Distilled millions of words

Brad continued to type research notes episodically into a series of Macintosh computers until he awoke one day to the fact that it was already seven years into the twenty-first century.

He wasn't going to live forever, so he started trying to organize into a book the millions of words he'd assembled on past InfoTech.

It's Brad's fondest hope that this book might entice scholars to delve deeper into the history of past InfoTech revolutions and perhaps uncover ways to avoid the pitfalls encountered in them.

He also believes college communications studies should require at least a one-semester course to instill a sense of the key roles information technology played in the rise of past civilizations.

About Michael Hart

Michael S. Hart was born March 8, 1947, in Tacoma, WA, and moved to Urbana, IL, in 1958, when his parents abandoned their business careers and decided to become professors.

At age eleven, having been taken to lectures and numerous other academic functions by his parents, Michael started to "drop in" to any number of classes at the University of Illinois and also to visit the departmental offices and ask for a "one-hour tour" of whatever subject interested him at the time. He was never turned down in such requests and thus continued to gain an education at the college level even when he was just finishing grade school.

The family home was filled with books, music, and artwork, and his parents studied diverse fields, ending up as full professors in math education and English literature. Not surprisingly, Michael's interests were equally diverse. He gives his parents high marks for raising him the best way possible, with freedom to roam both the educational and physical world, which resulted in him studying many subjects visiting all of the United States.

He didn't take to college life right away, nor did any of the four others in the famed "Class of '65," who in grades six through twelve took most of the advanced classes Sputnik (1957) had inspired.

All five found college not as interesting and dropped out. Hart gave it two tries in 1965 but complained that he wasn't learning anything.

The next five years include varied experiences. They included his first travel outside the United States and Canada and hitchhiking from coast to coast seven times in 1970, enough to get the Universe of Illinois to let him set his own curriculum, and he graduated in just two years with a straight-A average and a degree in "human-machine interfaces."

Early in those two years, he was drawn to the materials research computer lab, where he heard of the new network that became the Internet. Once again a hitchhiker, he was eventually given his own account and decided to "put something on the net that would stay for all time, millions of people would want, would be free of charge, and of great value," which he started with the US Declaration of Independence on July 4, 1971.

Three tries at grad school aborted, and Hart went back on the road until 1975. Returning to Urbana, he ran hi-fi shops from 1975 until 1988, when his interests started to turn more and more towards computers.

"Largest shoestring project in history"

While running a bicycle shop to support computer and bicycle habits, Hart received a request for a bike tune-up from a Benedictine monk. Soon, his connections with Benedictine University and the University of Illinois meshed and led to Hart's building the first physically accessible electronic library on the Benedictine campus and launching the Project Gutenberg Newsletter at the UI.

Project Gutenberg, which Hart calls "the largest shoestring project in history," already has enlisted perhaps a hundred thousand people to create eBooks. Today, the various Project Gutenberg sites around the world offer about a hundred thousand titles in many formats, all free of charge. Forty thousand of these titles were created inside Project Gutenberg, and many more were donated by various electronic libraries.

Hart looks ahead and envisions the possibility of translating each eBook into a hundred different languages. If only 40 percent of the public domain books were included, this would create a library of *one billion eBooks*.

Back to the present: Hart calculates if the average Project Gutenberg eBook eventually reaches just 1 or 2 percent of the world population, that would amount to a hundred thousand eBooks to a hundred million people.

This means that if the average Project Gutenberg eBook of today reaches only 1 or 2 percent of the world population, of which nearly three fourths has cellphone or computer, then Project Gutenberg has given away *ten trillion eBooks*!

Ten trillion eBooks given away by an organization that never has had a million dollars total over its forty year history ... all done by Michael Hart and his band of merry volunteers.

BIBLIOGRAPHY

Author's note:

The only originality in this book of any note is linking information technology revolutions to the reshuffling of power balances—first lifting Homo sapiens into dominance and then rearranging the power structure in one civilization after another.

As the Epigraph suggests, the book aims to attract others to seek to dispel more of the shadows that have hidden the history of previous InfoTech revolutions.

Rather than hoping to convince anyone of the truth of my conclusions, I hope others will challenge them.

Over the last half century, I tried to keep current a running file on "books I have read." I listed all those I recalled relating to this book and then sought the Highland Park Public Library Reference Department staff's help with publishers, dates, etc.

Here is the resulting bibliography:

Aurner, Nellie Slayton. *Caxton, Mirror of Fifteenth-Century Letters: A Study of the Literature of the First English Press*. New York: Russell and Russell, 1965.

Barnett, Linclon Kinnear. *The Treasure of Our Tongue*. New York: New American Library, 1967.

Blake, N. F. *Caxton, William (1415-24–1492): Oxford Dictionary of National Biography*. Oxford: Oxford University Press, 2004.

Bobrick, Benson. *Wide as the Waters: The Story of the English Bible and the Revolution It Inspired*. New York: Simon and Schuster, 2001.

Boorstin, Daniel J. *The Discoverers*. New York: Random House, 1983.

Broder, David. *Behind the Front Page: A Candid Look at How the News Is Made*. New York: Simon and Schuster, 1987.

Burke, James. *Connections*. Boston: Little Brown, 1978.

Cleaves, Francis Woodman. *The Secret History of the Mongols*. Cambridge, MA: Harvard University Press, 1982.

Cohen, Adam. *The Perfect Store: Inside eBay*. Boston: Little Brown and Co., 2002.

Diamond, Jared. *Guns, Germs, and Steel: The Fates of Human Societies*. New York: W. W. Norton and Co., 1998.

Durant, William and Ariel. *The Story of Civilization*. New York: Simon and Schuster, 1935–75.

Ehle, John. *Trail of Tears: The Rise and Fall of the Cherokee Nation*. New York: Doubleday, 1998.

Eisenstein, Elizabeth L. *The Printing Press as an Agent of Change: Communications and Cultural Transformations in Early Modern Europe*. New York: Cambridge University Press, 1979.

Follett, Ken. *Pillars of the Earth*. New York: Morrow, 1989.

Fuller, R. Buckminster. *Critical Path*. New York: St. Martin's Press, 1981.

Gassee, Jean-Louis. *The Third Apple: Personal Computers and the Cultural Revolution*. San Diego: Harcourt, Brace, Jovanovich, 1987.

Gladwell, Malcolm. *Outliers: The Story of Success*. New York: Little Brown and Co., 2008.

Crystal, David. *The Stories of English*. Woodstock, NY: Overlook Press, 2004.

Guillen, Michael. *Five Equations that Changed the World: The Power and Poetry of Mathematics*. New York: Hyperion, 1995.

Hawke, David Freeman. *Nuts and Bolts of the Past: A History of American Technology, 1776–1860*. New York: Harper & Row, 1988.

Hart, Mickey. *Drumming at the Edge of Magic: A Journey into the Spirit of Percussion*. San Francisco, CA: Harper San Francisco, 1990.

Hayakawa, S. I. *Language in Thought and Action*. San Diego: Harcourt, Brace, Jovanovich, 1990.

Hessler, Peter. *Oracle Bones: A Journey between China's Past and Present*. New York: HarperCollins, 2006.

Hogben, Lancelot Thomas. *From Cave Painting to Comic Strip: A Kaleidoscope of Human Communication*. New York: Chanticleer Press, 1949.

Hourani, Albert. *A History of the Arab Peoples*. Cambridge, MA: Belknap Press of Harvard University, 1991.

Illich, Ivan, and Barry Sanders. *ABC: The Alphabetization of the Popular Mind*. San Francisco: North Point Press, 1988.

Johnson, Haynes. *Sleepwalking through History: America in the Reagan Years*. New York: Norton, 1991.

Kaplan, Robert. *The Nothing that Is: A Natural History of Zero*. Oxford, NY: Oxford University Press, 2000.

Kernan, Alvin B. *Printing Technology, Letters, and Samuel Johnson.* Princeton, NJ: Princeton University Press, 1987.

Kincaid, C. A. *Successors of Alexander the Great.* Chicago: Argonaut, 1969.

Kluger, Richard. *Simple Justice: The History of Brown v. Board of Education and Black America's Struggle for Equality.* New York: Knopf, 2004.

Kluger, Richard. *The Paper: The Life and Death of the New York Herald Tribune.* New York: Knopf, 1986.

Kuhn, Thomas S. *The Structure of Scientific Revolutions.* Chicago: University of Chicago Press, 1996.

Kurlansky, Mark. *Cod: A Biography of the Fish that Changed the World.* New York: Walker and Co., 1997.

Laughlin, Robert B. *The Crime of Reason and the Closing of the Scientific Mind.* New York: Basic Books, 2008.

Lederer, Richard. *The Miracle of Language.* New York: Pocket Books, 1991.

Lewis, Bernard. *The Middle East: A Brief History of the Last 2,000 Years.* New York: Scribner, 1995.

Logan, Robert. *The Alphabet Effect: The Impact of the Phonetic Alphabet on the Development of Western Civilization.* New York: Morrow, 1986.

Lorayne, Harry. *The Memory Book.* New York: Ballantine, 1974.

Martin, Henri-Jean. *The History and Power of Writing.* Chicago: University of Chicago Press, 1994.

McCorduck, Pamela. *The Universal Machine: Confessions of a Technological Optimist*. New York: McGraw-Hill, 1985.

McLeish, John. *The History of Numbers and How They Shape Our Lives*. New York: Ballantine Books, 1991.

McNeil, William H. *The Rise of the West: A History of the Human Community*. Birmingham, AL: Gryphon Editions, Inc., 1989.

McNeill, William H. *Plagues and Peoples*. Garden City, NY: Anchor Press, 1976.

Miller, Kristie. *Ruth Hanna McCormick: A Life in Politics, 1880–1944*. Albuquerque: University of New Mexico Press, 1992.

Milne, A. A. *When We Were Very Young*. New York: Dutton, 1961.

Morgan, Elaine. *The Aquatic Ape*. New York: Stein and Day, 1982.

Orr, James McConnell. *Libraries as Communication Systems*. Westport, CT: Greenwood Press, 1977.

Papert, Seymour. *Mindstorms: Children, Computers, and Powerful Ideas*. New York: Basic Books, 1980.

Paulos, John Allen. *A Mathematician Reads the Newspaper*. New York: Basic Books, 1995.

Petroski, Henry. *The Pencil: A History of Design and Circumstance*. New York: Knopf, 1990.

Pinker, Steven. *The Language Instinct*. New York: HarperPerennial, 1995.

Ratchnevsky, Paul. *Genghis Khan: His Life and Legacy*. Oxford, UK; Cambridge, US: Blackwell, 1992.

Reid, T. R. *The Chip: How Two Americans Invented the Microchip and Launched a Revolution.* New York: Simon and Schuster, 1984.

Reid, T. R. *Confucius Lives Next Door: What Living in the East Teaches Us about Living in the West.* New York: Random House, 1999.

Roede, Machteld. *The Aquatic Ape: Fact or Fiction?* London: Souvenir Press, 1991.

Ryan, William and Walter C. Pitman. *Noah's Flood: The New Scientific Discoveries about the Event that Changed History.* New York: Simon and Schuster, 1998.

Seife, Charles. *Zero: The Biography of a Dangerous Idea.* New York: Viking, 2000.

Shlain, Leonard. *The Alphabet Versus the Goddess: The Conflict between Word and Image.* New York: Viking, 1998.

Shlain, Leonard. *Art and Physics: Parallel Visions in Space, Time, and Light.* New York: Morrow, 1991.

Simon, Irving Bernard. *The Story of Printing, from Wood Blocks to Electronics.* Irvington-on-Hudson, NY: Harvey House, 1965.

Smith, Richard Norton. *The Colonel: The Life and Legend of Robert R. McCormick, 1880–1955.* Boston: Houghton Mifflin Company, 1997.

Tawney, R. H. *Religion and the Rise of Capitalism: A Historical Study.* New York: Harcourt, Brace and Co., 1926.

Teilhard de Chardin, Pierre. *The Phenomenon of Man.* New York: Harper, 1959.

Temple, Robert K. G. *The Genius of China: 3,000 Years of Science, Discovery, and Invention*. London: Prion, 1998.

Wallace, James. *Hard Drive: Bill Gates and the Making of the Microsoft Empire*. New York: Wiley, 1992.

Weatherford, J. McIver. *Genghis Khan and the Making of the Modern World*. New York: Crown, 2004.

Wiegand, Wayne A. *Irrepressible Reformer: A Biography of Melvil Dewey*. Chicago: American Library Association, 1996.

Wenke, Robert J. *Patterns in Prehistory: Mankind's First Three Million Years*. New York: Oxford University Press, 1980.

The World Almanac and Book of Facts 1997

Index

Italic "*nn*" in page number indicates reference to footnotes

astronomers, 83
ATEX digital word processor, 125, 134
Atlantic Monthly (magazine), on enhancing memory, 133–134

B

Babylon
  creation of zero, 66–67
  temples of, 21
Bacon, Francis, 1
Baghdad, 40–42
Ballard, Robert, 16
Baltic Sea, 17
Bank of San Francisco, 102–103
Barnett, Lincoln, 71
Barnum, P. T., 112
BASIC (Beginner's All-purpose Symbolic Instruction Code), 132, 135–136
Basque fishermen, 61
Battle of Talas (751), 34, 40–42
Bell, Alexander Graham, 130, 131
Benedictine University, xi
Benton, Linn Boyd, 104, 104n22
best sellers, 83
Bible
  first English language printing of New Testament, 95
  first translation into English language, 93
  Gutenberg, 77–78
  reading among priests, 92
  using vellum, 32
black art, printing viewed as, 84
Black Death pandemic (black plague), 62, 75, 91–92
Black Sea, 15, 16
Blanc, Honoré, 88
block printing, 35, 62
Boleyn, Anne, 96–97, 97n21
book fairs, attracting print publishers, 83–84

bookkeeping, double-entry, 67–68
books
  affordability of, 78, 83
  digitalizing of books, 142
  empowering rise of mercantile class, 89
  Gutenberg Press and, 136
  Linotype impact on, 111
  19th century availability of, 99
  theft of, 75
Boorstin, Daniel J., 3, 13, 14, 57, 59, 61, 162
Boothy, Sir Brooke, 73
Boleyn, Queen Anne's Bible, 97
Braddock, Pennsylvania, first Carnegie public library in America, 119
brain
  evolving of, 9
  memory and, 13–14
breathing, controlling, 9
Britannia, 71–73
Brittannia's Golden Age, 72
British Empire, 97–98
British Isles, written language in, 71
British-Roman citizens, 72
Bush, George W., 139, 148
Bush, Vannevar, 133–134

C

Caesar, Julius, 71
Cairo, 40
calendars and centuries
Canterbury Tales (Chaucer), 94
Canute (Norse ruler), 73–74
capitalism, 62, 87–90
Carlos Magnus (Charlemagne), 43
Carnegie, Andrew, 115, 118–120, 119n27, 138
Carnegie public libraries, 119–120
Carnegie Steel Corporation, 118
Carolingian dynasty, 43
Carolingian miniscule script, 47

cathode ray tube (CRT), 2
Catholic Church, decline of, 149
Caxton, William, 93–95, 95n19, 138
cellular phones, 132
Celtics, 72–73
century, figuring out end of, 68
Cerf, Vint, 135
chalk and chalkboards, 130
Charlemagne, 43, 45
Chicago's World's Fair - Columbian
    Exposition (1893), 105
chimpanzees, 6
China
    developing pictographic languages,
        22
    in 14th century, 137–138
    Grand Canal of, 36
    papermaking in, 34
    printing in, 35–37
    supercomputers and, 40, 140
    writing in, 33–34
Chinese Imperial Palace, 37
Chinese ships, 31
Chinese writing, oldest written
    language, 33
Christianity and Islam, feud between,
    62
Christians, on parchment, 40
The Chronicles of England (Caxton),
    94–95
Church of England, 96–97, 96n20
church scribes, view of printing as
    black art, 84
Churchill, Winston, 72, 95n19
Classic Chinese, 33
clay tablets, 21–22, 32
Cleopatra, 32n6
Clinton, Bill, 139
*COD: Biography of the Fish that
    Changed the World*, (Kurlansky), 61
Cohen, Adam, 136
Columbian Library at Seville, 61
Columbus, Christopher, 37, 61, 73

Columbus, Ferdinand, 61
communicating, thoughts, 9
compass, invention of, 62
compressing, data, 134
computer keyboards, numerals on, 68
computer language, less technical, 132
computers
    analog, 131
    Apple II, 132
    Atlantic Monthly on, 133
    desktop, 138
    duplicating printers skills of,
        125–126
    first electronic, 131
    labtop, 138
    languages, 135
    Macintosh, 132
    Motorola, 132
    price of storage, 148–149
    Royal McBee LGP-30, 135
    single chip, 132
    storage, 148–149
    supercomputers, 140
    tablet, 138
Constantinople, 41–42
copy technologies, 132, 149
copyright
    acts, 146
    first law for, 145
    infringements, 141
Cordoba (Spain), 41–42
Court of Karakorum, 62
CPUs, 132
Crawford, Michael, 9
Crete, 40
*The Crime of Reason, and the Closing of
    the Scientific Mind* (Laughlin), 141
Cromwell, Oliver, 95n19
CRT (cathode ray tube), 2
cuneiform script, 21–22
cyberspace, 130

time line of revolutions, 143
in the West, 62
writing, 26, 33
integrated circuits, 132
intellectual property, vs. right to
knowledge, 141
intelligent design, power of speech
and, 7
interchangeable parts
capitalists profits and, 88
first use of, 87
International Monetary Fund (IMF),
140
International Typographical Union
(ITU), 111
Internet, 132, 134–135, 138–139,
146, 149
Irrepressible Reformer (Weigand), 116–117
Islam
empire of, 67
feud between Christianity and, 62
golden age of, 40–42
laws of, 39
mathematics and, 137
silk trade and, 59
Islamic scripture, 40
Italian, double-entry bookkeeping,
67–68

J

Jefferson, Thomas, 86, 150
Jobs, Steve, 150
judicial systems, built upon oral
decrees, 19
Jurched Dynasty
rule in China, 53
rule in Inner Mongolia, 53
rule in Manchuria, 53
justifying lines of text, manual process
of, 110, 110*nn*25
Jutes, invading, 72
Jutland (Danish), 72

K

Kahn, Bob, 135
Kalamazoo Gazette, 2, 125–126
Kemeny, John, 133–134
Kennedy, John, 135
Kepler, Johannes, book fairs and, 84
keyboard, of Linotype, 109–110
Khenti Mountain Range, 50
Khitans, 50
King Edward IV, 94
King James Version of the Bible,
publication in 1611, 97
kingdoms, limits of, 19–21
Kingsford, C. L., 95
Kluger, Richard, 103, 107, 111
knowledge
in Medieval Western culture, 82–83
sharing, 5–6
types of, 5–6
knowledge-sharing, 137–141
Koran, 39–42
Korean script, 35, 76
Koreans, 35
Kublai Khan, 57, 58, 60, 64
Kurlansky, Mark 61
Kurtz, Thomas Eugene, 135

L

labor union, war with Tribune, 104
labor unions, national printers union,
111
language
evolution of, 8
human life and, 10
origins of, 6
languages
oldest written, 33–34
tonal, 50
laptop computers, 138
laptops, 132
larynx, 11n3
larynx and speech, 8–9

World War I, 97
World War II, 97, 113, 131, 133
World Wide Web, 132, 138
Worms (Belgium), 95
Wozniak, Steve, 150
writing
    Chinese, 33–34
    impact of, 23
    phonetic, 26
    preserving original, 83
    replacing mnemonics, 21
    skills, 47
    symbols of shape, 137
writing surfaces
    before invention of paper, 31–33
    paper, 34–35
written language, in British Isles, 71
Wycliff, John, 91–93

X
Xerox machine, stiffing of, 146

Y
Yeke Mongol Ulus (Great Mongol
    Nation), 52

Z
zero
    creation of, 66–67
    hidden power of, 65–66
Zero, The Biography of a Dagerous Idea,
    (Seife), 23, 65–66